CN00656150

CARMEN

CARMEN

The life story of a true working lurcher

PHILIP GOSS

Published under licence by Brown Dog Books and
The Self-Publishing Partnership, 7 Green Park Station, Bath BA1 1JB

www.selfpublishingpartnership.co.uk

ISBN 978-1-78545-171-3

Printed and bound by CPI Group (UK) Ltd, Croydon CR0 4YY

Dedication

For Lynsey and Shaun:
I am so very proud of you both.

Acknowledgments
Cover artwork by David Rampling www.ramplingart.co.uk
Illustrations by Lisa Pope lisapopeart@btinternet.com
Thank you both for your help.

INTRODUCTION

Carmen came into my life in the summer of 1984. I had been looking for a bigger dog to join my kennel. Up until that time I had been almost purely interested in the pursuit of rabbits: the 22"-23" (to the shoulder) size of my dogs reflected this interest/obsession, with all of my dogs being rabbit specialists.

Lamping [rabbiting using artificial light] rabbits at night in particular had become such a big part of what I did that it dominated the majority of my thoughts, determined as I had been to take this interest to the extreme. One of my team of three rabbit-lamping dogs was in need of replacement, and my interest in including hare and fox into my nightly excursions was growing. In order to fill this void something bigger than my usual chosen type of dog was going to be required. Back in those pre-ban days I had a ready market for any hares that I acquired, being constantly asked by butchers to supply them, and fox pelts were making particularly good money.

Increasingly I appeared to be becoming known for doing a good job with rabbits and proving trustworthy: as a result of this, a growing number of farmers were making contact with me to ask me for assistance with controlling their foxes, especially immediately before and during lambing time. I liked to be able to offer this help free of charge, but in return for sole rabbiting permission on their land: this arrangement was proving a very successful way of extending the land I had permission to work on.

With all of these circumstances in mind I started to think about the type of dog I might like to consider bringing into my team. Back in those days lurcher puppies were not anything like as readily available in my area as they are today. Indeed, I believe that was true nationally: certainly in my area the type of dog that I had now decided to seek was unknown to me. Obviously I would need to go further afield. Adverts in what is now called *The Countryman's Weekly* (but back then was *Shooting News*) were watched, along with similar adverts in *Exchange and Mart* and the *Western Morning News.* Eventually after several dead-end enquiries, a litter was discovered in the Midlands: these sounded of great interest. A genuine-sounding person on the other end of the phone described how he would be keeping back two bitch pups from his current litter and selecting one for himself at a later date; I could have the other if I would like it. Both were rough-coated, both were orange brindle, and both were expected to make 25"/26" to the shoulder. For me at that time these represented monsters. Nevertheless, I was very excited by the discussion and felt confident that this was likely to be the right dog for me. They were collie/greyhound x deerhound/greyhound, or at least that's what he said they were: in truth they could have been almost anything and in all probability were a bit of most things, they were lurcher x lurcher. But despite the concern of whether these pups would indeed be right for me and after a two hundred and fifty-mile trip in a three-wheeler I was rewarded with the choice of two beautiful puppies of genuine quality. It turned out my new acquaintance had been unable to choose between the two and was perfectly happy for me to have either.

Together we discussed each pup and then agreed which would be mine. This had all happened on the day my sister joined the Navy, going aboard a ship called the *Carmen*. So with my Carmen loaded into the three-wheeler, the two hundred and fifty-mile trip home began.

Trust me, you have not lived until you have been overtaken by an HGV on the motorway whilst you sit helpless in a three-wheeler getting blown onto the hard shoulder as they pass; this surprisingly somehow soon becomes the norm, and equally surprisingly soon becomes perfectly acceptable and par for the course.

I survived the journey undertaken against all the advice of friends unable to understand why anybody would take on such a trip in such a vehicle just for a dog!

Carmen had travelled well and had slept nearly all the way. Now that she was at home I was so glad I had ignored all this so-called advice. I was so pleased with her: she was everything I had hoped she would be and more. At that time I had no idea just how lucky I really had been: I could never have imagined the life journey Carmen and I were about to go on together.

CHAPTER 1
TRAINING

In the early days after her arrival, Carmen lived indoors: eventually she would take her place in the kennel and live outside with my other two dogs, but as a young pup in a new home being unfamiliar with her future work and kennel mates, she was nowhere near being ready for anything like that at this early stage.

This arrangement was designed primarily for her benefit and safety, but also provided us with the perfect opportunity to spend one-to-one time together and start to get to know each other.

It was immediately clear that she had been well reared and looked after, as she was a very confident, outgoing pup. She was clearly not going to be readily fazed by anything; having said this, she also clearly preferred to be able to at least see where I was. If I went to a different room she was right there with me, so I considered her confidence to be nicely balanced: there was absolutely nothing about her manner that suggested to me that her training would be anything other than routine. Probably the most important thing at that early stage was that I really liked her and she was clearly happy to be near me.

I had the benefit of having trained several lamping dogs prior to Carmen's arrival, so having learnt from the many mistakes that I had made along the way, I felt that with this experience, coupled with such a lovely, level-headed pup such as she was to work with, we had a great chance together.

People seeing a well-trained lamping dog in action for the first time can be forgiven for believing that getting a dog to this high standard of efficiency is far harder than it really is.

Any fool can enter a field at night – and many do! – switch on a lamp and then allow their dog to pursue any illuminated rabbit. There is very little difficulty about that at all. But when you see this practice conducted properly, when you see a dog and its handler working together, both sides of the partnership knowing their respective roles, each side of the partnership trusting the other and knowing their job intimately, then it becomes a very different spectacle altogether.

To see a dog stand with its human partner watching the lamp sweep around the field searching; the dog's head appearing somehow as if it was connected to the light, so synchronised are its movements; the dog tensing up at the slightest moment's pause of the beam of light, thinking that something may have been spotted; the dog's instant reaction to being sent out when something has indeed been spotted; the spectacular manner in which each individual course is conducted; and then on conclusion of each run [course], successful or not, the light goes out and within seconds the dog is back at heel preparing to start all over again, having at times gently delivered its unharmed catch to hand; sometimes clearing a fence or a gate en route for good measure all without so much as a single word spoken, much of which will happen in total darkness – seems to the uninitiated to be well beyond the capabilities of an average dog trainer.

Well, it isn't, it is easily achievable for anybody who genuinely wants to succeed to this high standard and is prepared to put in the required amount of time and effort to form a foundation of trust between themselves and their canine partner, and having done so then help their dog through the different stages of what is nothing much more than an extension of basic obedience so that the dog knows exactly how to behave when its moment arrives.

I was more than ready to put in this effort, although I must be honest and say it hardly seems like effort when you enjoy doing it so much.

As soon as I knew that Carmen was happy to come to me – which was helped enormously by the discovery that she loved custard creams! – I started to play fetch with her with a rolled-up pair of socks. She loved this game and I could see that teaching her to retrieve was not going to be a problem. What this game also quickly revealed was that Carmen loved praise: if she thought she had been clever and was praised no matter how simple the task she had just accomplished may have been, she was beside herself with joy. We would play this game periodically through the day two or three throws at a time and then stop well before any type of boredom may have had a chance to affect her performance. Right from day one she was encouraged to come right back in with her retrieve and gently deliver it; this she was performing with an encouraging style even at this very young age.

Whilst she remained living indoors, as well as quickly learning what her name was, we also introduced both the sit and lie commands. All early success was rewarded and encouraged with a mixture of custard creams and praise, in no particular order.

Carmen's introduction to my other two dogs took place both away from their kennel and with Carmen safely in my hands. She was quite happy in their company and they in turn tolerated her keeping on with them in the way that only puppies can and invariably do. I suspect this toleration had a lot to do with them sensing that I approved quite strongly of our new team member and any objection from them would not be welcomed.

Once or twice Carmen did get put mildly in her place which I think seemed fair enough: she had to understand where she stood but fortunately the dominant bitch who had been my primary concern appeared to be the one that Carmen was most in tune with, so Carmen's early introduction to living with us could not really have gone much better.

Training a lurcher, I have always felt, can be divided into two categories: school/lessons and games/play. I think during each individual day certain times provide ideal opportunities to practise one from each.

School/lessons category would include lead training, walking to heel, sit, lie, stay – basically all the things that from choice a pup would prefer not to do.

Games/play would include retrieving and jumping, whilst remaining vital lessons for a working lurcher to learn they represent things that are of no particular hardship to a lurcher because they love to perform these disciplines. For naturally athletic lurchers these are simple, enjoyable tasks.

My method of training had become one from each category each day in order, and never moving on to the next until the first one was engrained. Having moved on, part of each subsequent training session would be spent revising the previously learnt lesson so that it was not possible for it to become rusty or get forgotten.

Carmen and I had approximately seven months to get to where we needed to be in readiness for her to start work, I expected and hoped for her to be ready at the age of approximately ten months old. This was a self-assessed target of when I expected her to be ready; it was not a fixed time, but it was what we would be aiming towards, so accepting this as a guide but little more, time was clearly on our side. Unlike the little pig who built his house of straw, we would be building our house of bricks, and we would utilise the time we had to the maximum. I would ensure that Carmen's foundation would be strong. Slow, steady progress is always the way with a running dog: they are not anywhere near the top of the canine intelligence league table – intelligence is not what they have been bred for – accepting this as a fact, they still have plenty enough intelligence to work with for the tasks we hope to train them to perform. Couple this with the obvious physical attributes they benefit from, and we have the perfect specimen for the job required.

By the time Carmen started to live outside in the kennel she knew her name and responded to it well: she would sit instantly, especially if a custard cream was involved; she would 'lie' and delighted in retrieving all manner of objects that were thrown for her, delivering them nicely and gently to hand.

Having moved her outside, I constructed a low fence that stretched from one side of my backyard to the other, a very low barrier that she would have to cross each time we went out. Every time she approached it I would say 'up' and before very long she would clear this with ease. We then started to practise retrieving over it: this she found as simple as a straightforward, normal retrieve, so the height of our barrier was increased in line with her capabilities but never in danger of exceeding them. I found watching her perform this exercise very exciting: everything about the fluent way in which she moved suggested to me that she had something a little special about her. I was genuinely thrilled by everything about her.

Training a lurcher to jump is quite a divisive subject, particularly amongst lampers, with many preferring that their dog does not jump for fear of it jumping into the unknown at night and risking serious injury or worse. Whilst I understand this sentiment I do not agree with it, and have personally seen far more injuries caused by dogs trying to jump something that they are not equipped to manage than I have dogs that have been encouraged and trained to jump, so enabling them to do so efficiently. Sadly, injuries happen as they do in any form of work or sport but each to their own: my dogs jump. Carmen would be equipped to jump when (and certainly not if) the time occurred.

Training over the barrier continued and very soon she would jump on command, regardless of whether we were going out or not: sometimes in order to accomplish a retrieve, sometimes just because she was asked to. My intention was to make sure by the time she was ready to start work that she could clear any five-bar gate or stock fencing. These were the kinds of obstacles that she would be confronted with almost every day of her working life: she would often need to get to the other side of these obstacles both quickly and unaided.

Hardly any gates or fences exceed 5' 6", so this was our benchmark: she was clearing 3' now with ease, so we were well on our way to gradually achieving our target.

In our early days I would take her out for exercise with the other two dogs. Leaving home in the van had meant that, aiming for rural surroundings, Carmen was not getting the opportunity to really meet other people, become used to traffic, or be on the lead for any significant period of time. Easily remedied but certainly not something to be overlooked.

Carmen was used to having a lead on: I had made sure of this, constantly putting it on for a short while each day and taking it back off again whilst she was still walking perfectly along beside me, releasing her from its restriction before she got fed up with it and risking its usage to descend into a war of wills and submission.

In order to give her the additional confidence of not being alone when confronted by significant traffic for the first time, I took the calming influence of the other two dogs with us. We went down towards the main road and held off about 50 yards back from the junction, choosing an expected quiet time for our first visit. I sat on a wall and Carmen was able to both see and hear cars going up the hill. The older dogs could see absolutely no point in what we were doing, but Carmen watched interestedly; she showed no signs of concern so we edged a little closer. Soon we were standing on the roadside with cars passing close by, but causing Carmen absolutely no concern in doing so. We returned home but repeated the exercise daily for the next three or four days. Eventually I took Carmen alone: cars, buses and lorries passed by but none caused Carmen any concern. In her working life she was only rarely going to come into contact with any form of traffic, but when she did I wanted to ensure that she was prepared for such an eventuality and anything else that she may encounter.

Carmen's training was progressing well: my previous experience of training dogs and her being a model pupil had meant that we were moving along nicely. This made it all the more surprising when we met our first problem. I had decided that we were ready to introduce the 'stay' command: I expected it to be accepted and dealt with in the same progressive way that all her other lessons had been dealt with. Nothing could be further from the truth. Carmen was evidently not a stayer: she really did not get it or did not like it, or perhaps a bit of both of this seemingly simple command. Eventually and reluctantly she would stay on command, but our first real hiccup to be encountered had been one of the last things that I would have ever expected to have caused her any sort of a problem.

Although Carmen's main purpose would be working at night where it was most unlikely that this command would ever be required, I knew that occasionally she would be working in the daytime with the ferrets, and on such occasions, particularly during our early forays, the 'Stay' command would become important and needed to be completely understood and obeyed. Having found a weakness, I felt we needed to spend longer on this lesson than I ordinarily would intend to do: we needed to eradicate it before we moved on.

Eventually, almost certainly due to this intensive training she received, Carmen 'stayed' as well as any dog I have ever owned. She responded perfectly by hand signal alone as she got older, but just how we had got there had not been at all routine.

Walking to heel was next added to our daily lessons. My command for this has always been 'get back'; my walking to heel does not necessarily meet with the criteria of most other dog trainers, particularly those that you see on the TV at Crufts: dogs pushing against the thigh of their handlers. This type of behaviour would be likely to result in any dog working at night either tripping its partner/handler up, or what would be far worse, getting its paws trodden on and potentially injured. So for me anywhere within about five yards equates to walking to heel: to the right, the left, or behind matters not, but never in front. I am perfectly happy for the dog to find its own path through woods or over rough ground at night in the darkness in areas where a lead is not practical. As I hold my lamp in my right hand – and I am a firm believer in the use of a slip lead whilst working at night – my dogs invariably tend to eventually naturally walk on my left, being so familiar with this being their position.

Carmen still needed to understand the meaning of 'get back'. This exercise I have always found to be one of if not *the* easiest, and is usually quickly understood. The dog is already walking nicely on the lead, so combining this with the command 'get back' does not require a great lot of ingenuity. As we progressed as usual before removing the lead I would spend a little time laying the lead on her back: this gives them the idea that they are still on the lead, which I guess effectively they are, but they are no longer under the handler's direct control: eventually the lead can be dispensed with, a lesson learnt in a similar fashion to a child learning to ride a bike with the use of stabilisers, removing them when you can already see that they are no longer required. Carmen had no difficulty in learning this important lesson.

Carmen was now about seven months old. She was already bigger than my other two dogs and was growing fast: summer had turned into autumn and the other two dogs were now working nightly when the moon was down and resting by day. This meant that Carmen and I were able to go out together one to one: these routine daily exercise periods were a perfect opportunity for us to practise and brush up on everything that she had been taught so far.

I took lamping rabbits very seriously and did not go out just for fun: I went out to do a job to offer a service and always tried my hardest to catch as many as possible. I could not put in all this effort alone and work with an unruly dog, they had to play their part: they had to give 100 per cent and respond instantly to any instruction. My expectations of the dogs were high, but in return I was prepared to put in the effort to train them to this standard, and I looked after them far better than I looked after myself.

All of Carmen's basic obedience was covered now: we just kept practising and improving response, which to be perfectly honest was already at a standard that I was more than happy with, but nevertheless we kept practising daily.

School/lessons: she responded instantly to her name and also a quick, pursed-lipped squeak. Sit, lie {down}, stay {with an upright stationary hand signal}, heel {get back}.

Games/play: the retrieve was moved from socks to ball to puppy dummy to normal dummy, to fur-covered normal dummy and now most recently dead rabbits and squirrels.

The command to carry out this task had turned from an excited 'fetch' to a whispered hiss, a sound that soon, when she started work and associated this sound with a rabbit having been spotted, would have an electrifying effect on her level alertness. Often during retrieving training a puppy, finding an object that it has been sent to collect far too easy to carry, will start to muck about with it. This occurrence demands that the weight is increased to make the pup more inclined to want to bring it straight back and relieve itself of the burden. Increasing this weight always troubles me with a young dog in that you may inadvertently make it a little too heavy and be encouraging the pup to naturally grip a little tighter, with perhaps the possibility of leading towards becoming hard-mouthed. When you are selling your catch of rabbits for financial gain, damaged rabbits are of course most unacceptable. Carmen fortunately never became affected by this often-encountered undesirable problem and always rushed back to receive the praise that she knew only too well would be waiting for her.

Jumping had progressed from yard barrier to all manner of various-sized walls, fences and gates. Carmen was also showing a good understanding of when something needed to be clear-jumped like a barbed wire fence, or when she could use the top as leverage like, for example, a solid, wooden-topped gate. In addition to this progress, I was in the process of teaching her to jump over my extended arm which I would lay on the top of any fence for her. This offered some temporary protection to her from the barbed wire that invariably ran along the top of most stock fencing. She was already getting the hang of this idea, something that could not fail to prove useful when we were out at work when circumstances allowed this method to be used.

Jumping and retrieving were often practised together: this was a perfect simulation of something that would certainly happen regularly when she was at work. Carmen loved this task, clearing with style any obstacle that had been carefully chosen for her, each obstacle always selected for being well within her capabilities, only increasing the height when it was known that she could definitely clear it. This in turn bred confidence as she had no idea what it was like to find it difficult to clear any obstacle, ignorant of the fact they had all been deliberately hand-picked for her: as a result, Carmen became a beautiful, confident jumper.

One thing that I was always careful of avoiding in these activities was ever allowing Carmen to be sent for something that she could not easily see. If she could not see it, the natural reaction would be for her to put her nose down and hunt for it, something to be avoided at all costs when training a rabbit-lamping lurcher. When she was working at night, in the event that she missed a rabbit I would want her to come straight back to heel as quickly as possible, not to start putting her nose down and start self-hunting under any circumstances. Should this inexcusable habit develop it would soon become a serious problem to us risking the potential of disturbing every rabbit in the field we were working. In time she would of course learn to use her nose, but not now if it could possibly be avoided. By the time she started to hunt in this way she should be so in tune with what we were doing at night and how to behave that she would understand when and when not it would be acceptable to use her nose.

The final lesson was what was and what was not acceptable to chase – as always, sheep being the primary concern. Having the other two dogs to help made Carmen's education absolute simplicity itself: on introduction to sheep Carmen showed no interest at all. I had regularly walked her near them and of course with her two mates ignoring them, that is what she instinctively copied and did. Eventually I went closer and closer with her until eventual she glanced their way and I was able to make her know that would not be acceptable. We made absolutely certain that this important fact of life for her was completely understood before she started working.

I felt quite certain that Carmen was now ready to be entered to rabbits; mentally I think she had been ready for quite a bit longer than physically, but now everything appeared to have come together and the time seemed right. I waited for the right night. Rabbits behave very differently in different weather conditions, some of which make it harder for the dogs to come to terms with the rabbits; others, like the night we had waited for, make it slightly easier.

The night Carmen started was dark, which sounds obvious, but dark as in no moon. This helps with the chance of approaching the intended target without either the dog or/and the handler becoming prematurely silhouetted, thus allowing the rabbits to detect any unexpected movement. It was windy which would baffle any possible sound from gates opening, whispered commands or approaching footsteps, and it was dry so the ground was not unnecessarily slippery for her on her first attempt. Perfect.

In addition to these favourable scale-tipping factors, I had already earmarked a small group of fields with a small number of rabbits living and feeding in each nicely spread out, which I had and always did leave completely alone in preparation for when I had a new puppy approaching this stage.

These fields favoured the dogs strongly in that the rabbits had to negotiate a good, solid bank that supported the dense hedge above in order to gain safety: to accomplish this they would have to slow down, and with a dog behind them not permitting them this luxury, they had a serious problem to deal with. These fields were both suitably sized and were perfectly level, so the chance of any selected rabbit being able to run into a non-illuminated area was non-existent. Carmen had everything in her favour exactly the right way to start an inexperienced pup. Had I gone into those fields with my other two dogs on that night, then confidence would have been extremely high. However, I knew from experience that with a young pup, despite all the careful planning, things could still quite easily go wrong.

We entered the field. Carmen was on a slip lead: this is a lead that in an instant will release the dog and yet holds it quite firm until the precise chosen moment arrives. Rabbits were immediately visible – at least to me they were. I could tell by the pressure on the lead that Carmen had not noticed them yet: that was perfectly expected, acceptable and in no way a problem. A few were feeding too close to the hedges to represent the individual we were searching for tonight, and further inspection of the field revealed that one had decided to squat further out towards the middle of the field: in lamping terms, 'squatting' means basically lying flat and quite still in an attempt to remain undetected. Very often this would be a successful ploy were it not for the rabbit's ruby-red eyes reflecting like a light in the beam of the lamp. This rabbit immediately became a very likely target: I moved into a position that I believed most likely would cut off this rabbit's intended eventual escape route should it change its mind from choosing to squat and bolt for home, knowing from experience this move, having being achieved, would hold this rabbit in its current squat position for longer than had we just directly approached it from where we, or rather I, had spotted it.

Having achieved our first objective and got ourselves into the perfect position, I started to hiss the sound that Carmen knew was asking her to go and retrieve. I could feel her head moving from looking around a little unsure of what was being asked of her to turning to look at me, presumably wondering what on earth I was making that sound for. We continued to make our way out to where the rabbit had chosen to squat, the lamp permanently on. As we got within 15-20 yards the rabbit's nerve gave and it broke for home. The pressure on the lead revealed that Carmen had seen it. I let her go immediately and she was away, she was on her first live run. The rabbit predictably led her to the hedge and then equally predictably became unable to slow down due to Carmen's close proximity and so was left with no other option but to turn and run up the side of the hedge. Carmen was closing on him fast when in an instant the rabbit changed direction and was returning towards where he had first been aiming for. Carmen could have been forgiven for losing sight of him at this point: this is a common occurrence in young pups and perhaps in the confusion the rabbit could have then made good his escape. In reality, though, this had not happened and she, too, had turned and was still very much in contention with a very realistic chance of making her first catch. The rabbit, due to Carmen's persistence, decided to try his same previously successful tactic again. This time, however, Carmen was a little further behind him, and so with the larger gap came a slightly longer length of time for Carmen to realise what was happening, adjust and react accordingly. This had proved to be an error on the rabbit's part and gave Carmen the opportunity to intercept him. With one decisive strike of her neck she lifted her first rabbit off the ground. Carmen barely broke stride as she brought her catch immediately to hand. She presented the rabbit to me in a way that I had always imagined that she would: we had strived for this from the very first time I had thrown a pair of socks for her. There was nothing that had happened that could possibly have been improved. One swallow certainly does not make a summer, but Carmen had caught her first rabbit in fine style and behaved impeccably throughout the whole exercise. All of our training had paid off: what she had done between being initially slipped and eventually catching the rabbit was purely down to her. That was totally reliant on her natural ability, but what she had done before and after those two moments was to have behaved in exactly the way that she had been trained to do. The result of this evening had been a complete success: Carmen had caught her first rabbit.

The actual spot where this incident happened is now years later buried beneath a supermarket floor on what is now part of a large industrial site. As sad as that is, I am quite sure that the people who push their trolleys up and down the aisles don't appreciate how lucky they are to walk on what is, thanks to Carmen, such sacred ground.

As soon as Carmen had her first catch we headed for home. I felt strongly that there was nothing to be gained by risking another run: for us to leave on a winning note and let the dog feel that it is unbeatable is the mentality I tried to install into all the pups I trained. I saw no point in risking trying the same thing again and tempting things to not work out in our favour the next time. Whether that was really necessary I cannot confirm, but I truly believed this to be the best way forward.

The following few nights we returned again and Carmen repeated her success: each time we caught a rabbit we went home. On the fourth night we carried on longer and Carmen caught three. She also missed one: this, of course, was an eventual inevitability but nevertheless an important moment in her education had occurred. As soon as I realised that she had missed it I called her, not caring about any of the other feeding rabbits that my call may disturb. It was important that she learnt to come straight back as soon as a run concluded, whether or not it was in our favour. This she unsurprisingly immediately did, and for doing so she received praise very much on a par with that which she would have received for making a catch. A dog that can be trusted to come straight back in the darkness on concluding a run is most desirable: you can immediately reorganise and try again. Often rabbits feed in close company and a well-trained dog behaving in this way can competently pick them off one at a time, whilst a poorly trained dog would have probably sent them all running for home.

Carmen's basic training was complete and now she was also entered to rabbits. She had much too still learn, but now her education would be taken further by experience alone: whilst working, she would learn the tricks of the trade. She would learn about how I worked and I would learn about her. Each dog is an individual, and a handler that is not prepared to vary his/her technique when necessary to accommodate his/her canine partner's peculiarities is almost certain to be restricting their own success. Each dog has weaknesses that we need to identify and find a way around, and each dog has strengths that we need to capitalise on. I was very excited about forging a partnership with Carmen and was very confident in where we were going by the time she stepped up and joined the other two dogs as a full part of our rabbit-lamping team.

Carmen aged 10 months old

CHAPTER 2
RABBITING YEARS

Carmen stepped up to join the other two dogs as part of the rabbiting team. I had become very excited about the early signs of her potential. She was already showing a maturity and a wisdom way in advance of her age, and seemed to be learning very quickly. Her eventual role was intended to enable me to realistically target the hares and foxes that I was regularly asked to control, and for which I had a ready market. This, however, was for later; to start with, I intended to keep rabbits as her main quarry and let her serve an apprenticeship on something that was easily within her capabilities before stepping up to the much more athletic hares and the more formidable foxes.

A dog entered to hare prematurely could easily become despondent and lose confidence in its own ability, having been outmatched by the hare's superior running ability. On the other hand, should a young dog be fortunate enough to take a hare, which is far from impossible, with conditions heavily favouring the dog, how then to deal with this strong animal on capture becomes an issue for the youngster. I always feel this only encourages the dog to start thinking about squeezing a little to gain control with the possibility of becoming slightly hard-mouthed an obvious reality, something I constantly feared and would want to avoid at all costs, supplying, as I was, the local butcher's who I am quite sure would have looked elsewhere for their supplier had our standards dropped.

Foxes, on the other hand, are certainly far easier to come to terms with than the hare for any lurcher, but foxes have the capability to retaliate. I am quite sure many potential fox dogs were ruined by being entered too soon: a youngster getting bitten being often put off from ever tackling this quarry again, made nervous of risking any chance of a repeat performance in the future. Faced with a similar situation, an older dog would be much more inclined to make a good account of itself, particular a dog that has been brought on in a sensible manner and allowed to progress at a speed dictated by its individual capability, not by any foolish comparison to others.

Each dog is different and there will always be exceptions to any rule, but I had firmly decided that Carmen would start her working life on rabbits and then proceed accordingly.

At twelve months old I was sure that she had stopped growing. She now measured 25½" to the shoulder: she was very strong with particularly strong shoulders, a powerful back, and enormous back leg muscles. Her feet were compact and her toes nicely boxed and not at all flat. She had a long neck and when she moved it was pleasing to the eye: she flowed, and everything moved smoothly together. Carmen's coat was rough, wiry as opposed to soft, and her skin seemed strong and thick, a massive plus in a working dog, particularly one that would be working at night, regularly diving head first into thick hedges and often coming into contact with the scourge of all lampers: barbed wire.

Early lamping trips with any pup were always carefully selected so as to never put the youngster in a position where it did not have a realistic chance of success. Fields where the fleeing rabbits were likely to go over a slope into the shadows were avoided, fields where the rabbits may run straight into cover with no hedge to help the dog, fields where the hedges were so loose that, again, a rabbit was able to gain entry without slowing down – these are examples of places where a young dog will be hugely disadvantaged. Yes, they will occasionally catch but these places do nothing to build the confidence in the dog to the level I used to try and achieve. Youngsters who catch most of their early efforts really start to believe in themselves. The confidence is quite visible. Gradually, of course, all of these earlier unfavourable conditions will in time be attempted, but for me not before I knew my dog was in the right frame of mind and ready for them.

Carmen was no exception: our early nights out together were always on good ground, strongly favouring her. She was showing early signs of having remarkable agility for a dog of her size, which took me by surprise. I was perfectly prepared to accept that in choosing a dog of her breeding I was going to have to forfeit some agility to acquire the size and power I was seeking. Somehow everybody had seemingly forgotten to tell Carmen of this accepted compromise. She single-handedly set about trying to prove everything I thought I knew to be wrong. When her rabbit turned she was right with it; she ran with her head held very low when in close proximity to her target; when the rabbit made the slightest mistake it paid for it; if the rabbit ran straight she just picked it up; if it turned to try and avoid capture, her reflexes were such that she would make snatching it up appear the simplest thing in the world. Should the rabbit reach cover, she dived in as if her life depended on it, and far more times than not extracted it. Whatever was required she was more than prepared to do. Having made her catch she then retrieved it to hand at a speed very similar to what her outrun had been, much faster than I had ever been used to, with the benefit of her additional size I didn't even have to bend down to receive her catches, she just placed them straight into my standing hand and was ready to go again.

It was impossible for me not to start fantasising about what Carmen was possibly going to be capable of as time progressed: I had never seen or owned a dog with such natural talent. I had always been and would always remain very proud of all the other dogs I had, or had previously owned and worked with. I would never criticise any one of them, they all gave their best: some were better than others. All had strengths and all had weaknesses, but none, however, was anything like Carmen. She appeared to be the full package.

Personally I had sacrificed what perhaps for many may have been termed a normal youth for my era in order to follow my heart. I loved to be out alone at night: the thrill, the challenge, the satisfaction, the feeling of being the only one alive – nothing could dissuade me. The rain, the wind, the cold: I loved it all. My friends said I was mad and it was not possible to live like that: this just made it even more certain that I would.

I saw no need for their fashionable clothes. I saw no point in mundane jobs to earn a wage spent on alcohol, flashy cars and going out to places where I never wanted to be or felt uncomfortable in.

I would not have their wealth, I accepted that, but none of them would have my freedom or happiness. I was certain that I had the better deal.

Having made these calculated decisions and being determined to turn them into a success, more and more I scrutinised my lamping method and technique. I tried to take everything, no matter how seemingly small it may be, to the limit. Practically every waking thought was spent on where I would be going that night, memorising routes, gaps, gates, fences, anything for me to get the dogs into the right place to give them the best possible chances of success.

If the time and effort I put into my chosen lifestyle were converted into a financial hourly rate, then my salary was very poor, but if it was converted taking into account the degree of happiness I maintained, then I really was extremely well off. I absolutely loved it.

One of my constant considerations was deciding which dog to use on any individual night, trying to match the resources available to me to the ground we would be working on. The dogs I had at this time, though both fully committed to their job, were so very different in running style. Tina, primarily of greyhound/whippet blood, was very fast, very direct, extremely agile and skilful: she could snatch rabbits up from almost any angle and would soon amass a very respectable night's bag. Her weaknesses were that her courage and commitment were not enclosed in a body built to sustain the knocks and bumps a lamping dog must endure, so injury was all too frequent. Her stamina also proved restrictive: her strike rate was so high that she took the type of numbers that were hoped for, but she did have a tendency to run out of steam. This is something that, if ignored, could prove very serious; in such cases I believe the handler has a duty and must recognise the moment when to stop for the dog's own safety. The dog will invariably want to keep on going, having no regard for its own well-being, very much in a similar way to that of a boxing trainer who may throw in the white towel contrary to the fighter's wishes.

Tess was the dominant bitch in the kennel. Tess was basically a mongrel of no particular breeding: she clearly had running dog in her, but it was equally obvious that a strong dose of collie blood ran through her veins. I had seen Tess as a puppy walking along the road with a lady beside her owner's pram clearly having been bought as a pet. I admired her and thought it to be such a shame that a dog like that was condemned to spend her life trotting beside a pram. One morning a knock on the door from a friend who also enjoyed a night's lamping revealed the story that he had, unknown to me, bought this particular bitch – for a pint! – off her drunken owner in a local pub and had had her for several months, but things were not working out for them and so she was now being offered for sale because she was 'rubbish'.

A night was organised to go and watch her in action. She was confused and was making really strange decisions that were indeed reflecting very badly on her, but if what I thought she was doing was indeed what she was doing, the reasons these mistakes were being made would prove very successful when eventually, or indeed if ever, perfected.

A rabbit would be spotted, Tess would be slipped, and all too often she went completely the wrong way. Several demonstrations resulted in the same almost comical outcome. "You see, rubbish," my frustrated friend declared. "What are you asking for her?" I enquired, knowing full well she had been bought for the equivalent of less than one pound. A price was suggested despite her being 'rubbish': her value, it appeared, had seemingly escalated! "I will buy her from you," I replied. This took my friend by surprise and he questioned my reasoning. I refused to offer an explanation and just repeated my willingness to pay the full, inflated asking price (which for me at that time, being practically penniless, was quite an outlay): I liked her. Suddenly Tess was no longer for sale: "if you want her I am keeping her," came the response. The night ended and my friend left with his dog. About a fortnight later, his frustration having got the better of him, he returned. "Do you really want this dog?" he asked. I did and Tess came to live with me.

Tess had had a very disrupted start to life: she was still little more than a pup. With patience and time to work out her ways, she did indeed perfect her unusual style and became a valued member of my team. She caught some enormous hauls of rabbits: her strengths and weaknesses were almost the complete opposite of Tina's. I often thought of how it would have been if you could have merged them into one.

Eventually I settled on the abandonment of my one-man, one-dog policy and used to work them together, one off and one on the lead. Only ever having one dog running at any given time, this required both dogs to have instant obedience and full respect for each other. The benefits to me for this additional complication was that I could now develop a system which allowed me to use each dog in its own respective area of strength and match the dog to the ground for individual runs, as opposed to whole nights. In areas where both were equally suited, they would take one field each at a time and then swap as we passed through the gate into the next field.

It worked for us and we managed; it was not easy, especially when we were enjoying a productive night and had no place to drop off our catch for future collection, and so had to keep it with us. But I took my time: we had plenty of that and slowly, methodically progressed through the night.

What was now becoming increasingly apparent was that in Carmen I now had a dog that not only shared my attitude towards what we did but, it appeared, encompassed everything that my other two dogs shared between them and more. She appeared determined, completely unable to even contemplate giving up, intent on breaking all the rules of what was and was not possible. She appeared to have all of Tina's skill and style; she also, it appeared, had all of Tess's intelligence, stamina and robustness. Her size gave her more strength, and she was faster. I used to stand and look at Carmen and think that if this dog has a weakness I can't see it. I could not help but get carried away with my excited optimism for our future together.

Carmen's nights out were gradually being extended in line with her progression; she learnt very quickly and in truth I probably held her back a little, determined, as I was, that she should not suffer a setback. She clearly loved what she was doing and was always saddened when left at home, deemed to be not quite old enough yet to take on a whole night. Her sessions where either short trips to ideal places early in the evening before myself and the other two dogs went out for the full night, short trips late when the moon was rising, or early when it was falling. During these times a perfectly adequate period of time could be set aside for her, and how she loved them.

One evening a friend not seen for quite some time knocked on the door to say he had a young dog that he was taking out and would I like to come and watch it perform? This friend had a long-standing interest in rabbiting, but I had not realised that he had acquired a lurcher: he had always tended to ferret and shoot.

Several years previous to this he had asked if he could come out and watch the dog I was running at the time work. Of course he could, if only just for a few runs. Having slipped the dog on the first rabbit of this particular evening, this individual started to chuckle, at what I had no idea: each successive time the dog turned the rabbit, the laughter grew more uncontrolled. Eventually this made me laugh, this soon snowballed and resulted in us both falling into hysterical laughter which persisted and increased until the dog eventually took the rabbit and started to bring it back. I had no idea why I was laughing. It turned out that he could not really offer any kind of explanation why he was laughing: either it just appeared to be a strange, involuntary reaction to the spectacle he saw. I think to this day in my experience that remains the strangest reaction to seeing a lamping dog at work for the first time.

He came in and discussed where he was going and soon we agreed that Carmen would come with us: she had never been out with another dog before, and I was interested to see how she behaved and also felt it a good opportunity to extend her education. The farm we were heading for was well known to me, and the ground it was on should in no way trouble dogs of Carmen's age and level of experience. My colleague's dog was, although young, several months older than Carmen and from what he said quite a bit more experienced.

We arrived at the farm, having already agreed to run the dogs alternately run for run. I informed him that if I felt that any run was not acceptable to Carmen I would let him know and we would forfeit our turn, rather than risk any possible avoidable miss. He mocked my protective attitude towards Carmen and I in turn ignored his ignorance.

The back of the van opened and his dog was immediately gone into the darkness. He repeatedly called its name but it didn't appear to know it, or perhaps it was deaf? Carmen jumped out and stood beside me and I slipped the lead over her head. "She will be back in a minute," our friend declared. Investigation with the lamp did not support his claim: she was nowhere to be seen. Eventually his dog did come back into sight, and after quite a bit of coaxing and deception she was captured and we were at last ready to go. This was going to be an interesting evening. Inside, unspoken, I had already decided that if Carmen as much as looked like she may be tempted to copy this unruly dog, I would come back to the van immediately.

I had no reason to fear: she behaved impeccably, she acted with such maturity, and she completely ignored everything bad that went on around her. This friend's dog was not in any way ready to be out at night: it had no level of obedience. It had no idea what it was doing, and I am afraid finding who was responsible for putting it into that situation was very easy. I liked this person but he had let his quite nice little dog down badly. I persevered with the evening for longer than I normally would have under the circumstances because I felt that this was revealing another side of Carmen that for obvious reasons I had never seen before.

She was never tempted to participate in any of the other dogs' antics: she very independently behaved perfectly and I was so proud of her. I refused point-blank to help this friend recapture his dog whenever it was off the lead: that dog was not my concern. I focussed totally on Carmen and repeatedly quietly praised her for her behaviour.

The evening drew to a close and we never went out with that person again: what became of that unfortunate dog I have no idea.

Incidents like that helped remind me of how I had developed such a strong preference for lamping alone. I worked where I wanted and how I wanted; my dogs behaved how I wanted because I would teach them. I cannot honestly remember ever needing to tell any dog off out lamping. I remember plenty of praise and admiration offered their way, but if they had ever done something wrong that would have been my fault for not teaching them properly and I could never have accepted that from myself.

Carmen continued to go from strength to strength and the shackles were now off: she was undoubtedly ready for more than she had been offered up to this point. I remember sitting before leaving home on one particular night thinking how this was the case and deciding to see what she could really do. I would keep a careful watch and stop if there was the slightest sign of any kind of problem, but short of that it was over to her.

The route I decided to take was a favoured one and held a good number of rabbits and had proven successful on numerous occasions. The ground was mixed, there were plenty of good puppy-type fields, but equally there were areas where even the most experienced dog may find life difficult. Providing the night was progressing well, Carmen would be allowed to take on any run that we were presented with.

That night, more than any other before it, confirmed what I had suspected for so long: she superseded every expectation I had and took by far the largest haul from that ground than I had ever achieved before. The number of rabbits we actually saw was in line with what was expected, but her strike rate was extraordinary. It did not matter to Carmen what the ground or situation was, she seemed to be able to adapt and apply the appropriate tactic for the individual run taking place. If a rabbit looked likely to run over a hill and out of the light, she rushed in and put everything into one big, determined lunge. Should a rabbit be against a hedge she would apply enough pressure to make the rabbit turn, but she would have stayed far enough back to react to this anticipated move and pick him up with contemptuous ease. This was a dog in total control of what she was doing. This is what she was bred for, this is what she had been trained for, but now it was over to her: nobody else could take credit for what she was displaying. This was Carmen. I had never seen anything to this standard before, and alone in the dark struggled to contain myself with a mixture of excitement, pride and above all admiration. I had dreamt that a dog like this could exist without truly believing that it could, and now she was here with me in the early hours of the morning being given her opportunity to shine, just treating it as if it was nothing, as if it was easy – what is all the fuss?

During our early lamping trips Carmen had seen plenty of squatters, but had never been allowed to attempt any target unless it was moving. Carmen's targets were always on the run at this time: by the pressure on the lead you know exactly when the dog you are with has seen the focus of your attention. Through this you are able to determine the precise moment to release the dog. It may be, for example, that you need to get to another position in the field before releasing the dog to avoid the prospect of the rabbit running unavoidably out of the beam; by the time you have achieved that objective and gained this position you may then decide that the rabbit is now too near to safety to allow the dog a realistic chance of making a catch. The dog is not released and an alternative target searched for. That to me is far preferable to taking a chance that most times – not always but most times – will end in failure for a young dog.

Having made such an impression under these guidelines and going by her reaction to when a squatter became noticed, I was certain Carmen was ready to start giving them a try.

The skill of taking squatters to a rabbit controller has massive implications: a dog that can do this efficiently under the right conditions will greatly influence the night's bag. To someone out to simply give their dog a run or two, the taking of squatters may seem a little unsporting. Strangely, I think the best way of teaching a dog to take squatters is to not let them do it, and that is exactly how Carmen learnt this discipline.

With a squatter found, the light was left on continually as we walked towards it: the whispered hiss that she now knew only too well meant that something for her to go and catch had been spotted was also continually sounded. Eventually one of two things would happen: either the rabbit would lose its nerve and bolt for home, in which case the chase was on, or the rabbit would sit perfectly tight until we got right up to it, only running for home when we were right on top of it: again the chase was immediately on. Each time this happened, Carmen was learning that the object in the centre of the beam was indeed a rabbit. Each time it happened, I could feel through the lead the level of understanding of this important lesson. When I was absolutely certain that the penny had dropped I allowed Carmen to try catching a few before they moved. The danger at this time is being fooled into thinking that the dog has seen the rabbit when really it has not; you must be certain that the dog is actually focussed on the rabbit and not some other foreign object which just happens to be nearby. The best way of ensuring this is to only let the dog try for squatters that you are right on top of to start with. At this moment in this position you have the best possible chance of being sure that you are both on the same page.

Predictably, given how everything else with Carmen had gone, she took to this practice with flying colours. Her style with squatters was very direct and very precise – no mucking about, racing straight in, and one accurate strike of her neck and a whole lot of her energy was instantly saved. Gradually, once this stage had been reached and she had been successful on several occasions, I started to allow her to run a longer distance to the squatter. It was lovely to see her using the beam of light. I had taped the lamp in to create a pencil-thin beam: this prevented the whole field being disturbed as we worked. Carmen worked with this beam perfectly. Sometimes I would slowly arc the lamp around the field and watch her head: it was as if the two were directly connected, so synchronised were their movements. As time progressed I would send her for a squatter perhaps at distance, and I could see that she had not actually pinpointed exactly where it was but she trusted me, and if I sent her she went, but I could tell the moment she had actually saw it for herself. Her shoulders went down, an unspoken way of recognising the moment when her body would be saying, OK, I have got this, leave it to me!

Occasionally Carmen would accidentally run past the squatter, failing to notice it as she passed. This can often happen in certain places: amongst molehills, for example, or in amongst bare patches of an otherwise grass field, tucked in behind a clump of grass. All these things are examples of where a squatter can become camouflaged from the dog's view. A dog's view is very different from ours: try crouching down to their height and see what they see; it can be noticed how ours, elevated as it is, is a very privileged, much clearer view.

When Carmen had overshot her target I would lower the lamp so that the target rabbit was right on the extreme fringe of the circle of light: much of the grass between the rabbit and myself would become illuminated. Carmen would at this moment become invisible; she soon learnt what this meant and within a few seconds her eyes would light up, telling me that she had turned around, realising she had gone too far. Incidentally, at this time when her eyes lit up in this way, Carmen had one orange eye and one that shone blue. Having turned around she would start to walk back towards me always in the centre of the beam, always staring intently at the ground in front of her and between us knowing what she was looking for was very close, she would soon spot it. I would help guide her in using the light to direct her and she would then quickly pick it up.

Carmen had learnt what for us was a very important lesson, one that, once learnt, would now never be forgotten and she was now performing it expertly on an increasingly regular basis.

At this time, thanks to Carmen, life took a turn for the better. My outgoings remained the same and yet my income increased to the point where I actually had more than enough to survive on, as opposed to having barely enough. My local butcher's could not keep up with Carmen, though, and I had to go further afield to dispose of our catches for the first time ever. I had entered a real purple patch in my rabbiting career. I had for so long felt the mainstay of our rabbiting team, but now I genuinely felt that I had to up my game to keep up with her. I had imagined for so long what it would be like to have a dog capable of attaining the standard that Carmen had already surpassed, but I had never really believed it could be possible.

Carmen continued to perform to her increasingly high standards and in doing so had almost caused me to forget the real reason I had originally wanted a dog of her size to join our team. Now I had a real dilemma: I had butchers wanting hares, and farmers expecting me to offer some form of protection to their lambing fields in return for the rabbits they had permitted me to have. But the dog I had brought in for this very purpose had now become without any doubt whatsoever my number one rabbiter. I considered each contributory factor to this awkward decision, and the one overriding concern that kept becoming the one obstacle I could not get past was my fear that, should I start to run her on these bigger quarry species, would she start to get hard-mouthed? Carmen was so beautifully soft-mouthed with her rabbits that when they were skinned you would be forgiven for assuming that they had been netted: they never bore a mark.

After much thought a decision was reached: I was duty-bound to help the farmers with their foxes, but I could take care of that by snaring. The hares would be left alone and the butchers would just have to find another source. Carmen was going to carry on in her rabbiting ways. I was not prepared to risk sacrificing her exceptional ability in this field for anything or anybody.

So continue we did night after night, rewriting our own personal record books each time we went out. Carmen seemed to become even more accomplished, she was a master of her craft, and she would seemingly always find the right way to tackle any and each individual run. Rabbits that now ran out of the beam, over a hill or slope into the shadows were no longer assured of their safety: she regularly disappeared over my horizon out of view only to return shortly afterwards carrying her catch. Really the only rabbits that had a realistic chance of avoiding her accurate strike once she had zeroed in on them were ones who were fortunate enough to live on ground that strongly favoured them; this was in no way certain to save them, but for the rabbits she got behind on favourable ground to her, the conclusion of the run was almost inevitable.

Her ability was coupled with my experience of the ground we worked. I was able to get her into optimum position to succeed. Which way to lamp each field was memorised, where to stand to get the most beneficial results. We worked with the wind in our faces wherever we could. Rabbits close to us were taken first, only later searching further out into the field: trying to keep this type of order gave us a maximum number of runs per field. Squatters were picked off, again nearest first. One night Carmen took five squatters one after the other in a matter of a couple of minutes; all had been feeding in close proximity to each other yet with the wind, slightly taller than normal grass and Carmen's obedience, retrieval speed and understanding of what we were doing, she caught them all. A couple of moments like that in any night can soon make a world of difference to the bag [number of rabbits in total], whilst the dog's energy and battery power usage are minimal.

I remember one night years before when I had been in the process of entering a puppy named Merlin, a non-lamping friend had been persuaded to come out with me and hold the pup whilst I ran Tina to allow the pup to watch what went on. On our way home from our very short trip this friend remarked how he preferred it when Merlin was running, as he felt at least the rabbit had a chance, as opposed to when Tina ran, who he felt was like watching Liverpool (the football team who were winning everything at that time): you knew what the result would be as soon as she got started.

So it was with Carmen: goodness only knows what he would have thought of her. She so rarely made a mistake and her level of application was intense. One night she had caught a rabbit in a very standard manner. I switched the lamp off as always and waited for her to return with it; the rabbit had been some distance from us, but nevertheless she appeared to be taking longer than the anticipated time to return. Deciding to check on her progress, I flashed the light on to see that she was indeed almost back, but in turning on the light I caught a glimpse of a rabbit racing across the illuminated ground between us. Carmen also saw it and immediately set off in pursuit. More due to astonishment than anything else, I left the light on to see how she thought she was going to manage to pick up this rabbit whilst still carrying the very live original rabbit in her mouth. The rabbit was turned once and Carmen was right behind it. They were very close to me as the rabbit attempted to make good his escape up the side of the banked hedgerow. Carmen followed and suddenly pinned the rabbit against the bank with one of her front legs. I rushed in and helped her and we caught the pair of them. I had never seen a dog do anything like that before; had I not been so close I suspect the second may have got free, so there were circumstances that contributed to this seemingly impossible scenario, but Carmen had caught two at a time! I must confess that if I was told that story I would struggle to believe it possible, but somehow – maybe because of my total admiration for all that Carmen was proving capable of – it did not seem at all surprising.

One night a lamping friend came around to say that he had been asked to help out with the rabbits on a distant farm. He had already visited this particular farm and found that the farmer's report of being overrun with them was for once true and accurate. Many farmers seem to feel overrun at the sight of a rabbit on their land and are inclined to overexaggerate their personal rabbit problem. Anyway, this one apparently had not: I was asked if I would be prepared to help.

I strongly preferred my own company when lamping, but the temptation of getting access to this reported type of population was far too strong, I know that my real response should have been that I was only too happy to help a friend in need, but that would be a lie, it was the thought of being amongst big numbers of rabbits that encouraged me to agree to his request.

The night we chose to visit this farm for the first time together was perfect for what we were doing: dark, dry and windy. He had his own dogs of which he brought one, and naturally Carmen was the one that I had chosen to accompany me. His dog was vastly experienced and so the standard practice of running the dogs run for run was agreed to be adopted. As soon as we started we were in amongst them: there were a lot, but strangely I felt it was clear from how the rabbits behaved that they had not been lamped before, so this farmer must have ignored his problem for some time before finally deciding to address it.

We made a good start with both dogs doing their job. It was not long before my colleague remarked on Carmen – from someone who actually knew what he was doing, this was considered a compliment indeed. The first thing he remarked on was how quick Carmen caught her rabbits: no repeated up and down hedges for her. Usually Carmen's rabbits were a run of one turn and strike and she was quickly on her way back. The second thing he commented on was the speed of the retrieve. I could tell he was genuinely surprised. I thought that what had probably contributed to his surprise was that I had not mentioned anything to him previously regarding her ability, not deliberately but

Carmen's ability had not been raised in our conversation and I felt no reason to bring it up, knowing that he would see for himself anyway.

We carried on and were amassing quite a number: Carmen had contributed just under two-thirds of the bag. I knew this exactly because I was quietly keeping count; it was in no way a competition but I was interested to see how she did compared to another experienced dog on identical ground running run for run. Whatever the night's bag proved to be, it would be split 50/50 irrespective of which dog caught them: that had already been agreed. We stopped for a break and paunched our catch so far whilst enjoying a cup of tea from a thermos before going on again. I felt my colleague's dog was starting to falter: she certainly was not catching as frequently as she had been earlier in the night. I mentioned my suspicions, but my colleague did not share my opinion. We carried on, and just a few runs later it became obvious that she needed to stop: she was spent. We walked back to the van which she comfortably managed where we gave her food and drink. She jumped up into the strawed back of the van and was evidently very tired but fine. My colleague asked what I wanted to do. I saw no need for any concern for his dog: I had seen dogs like this and far worse many times before, especially Tina, and knew that all she needed she had been given. My wish was to carry on, but if he wanted to call it a night I understood, and in that case that is exactly what we would do.

"What about your dog?" he enquired. "She is fine," was the reply because that genuinely was the case: Carmen had plenty more to give. I would have never dreamt of pushing Carmen beyond her capabilities: there was no fear of that.

We carried on, Carmen now totally in charge of proceedings. Carmen was fit, very fit, and was now benefiting from how her catching ability saved her energy. She had not worked anything like as hard as my colleague's dog and yet had caught so many more. This had not gone unnoticed by my colleague and he was not slow in voicing his admiration for her. Carmen was relentless and after we had completed our night's lamping she was still in a position to carry on further if required. There was no need to carry on: we had had a fantastic night, and we circled back to the van where my colleague's dog, having been given time to recover, was now delighted to see us and found to be clearly feeling better. The rabbits were paunched and counted: Carmen had now contributed just over three-quarters of the catch. Which was her new individual record. We loaded up and set off for home. Carmen was the topic of our discussion as we travelled; the conversation then led to my colleague asking how much I would sell her for. He knew, he said, that he could not afford her; he was not asking to buy her but felt, with every dog having a price, that he was interested to know how much would someone have to offer to prise her away from me. He received an instant answer: I would never even think of selling her.

As we travelled I sat and thought about that question, having never once even considered the prospect before. I was financially poor but I knew that, no matter what, I would never even think of allowing someone to take Carmen away. If something was to happen to her my world would collapse. I had very little in the way of possessions; Carmen was the one thing that I genuinely treasured. We arrived home, my colleague still convinced that I would sell her to the right offer. We agreed to go back to the same farm together.

The following week we set off together again: this time, however, we were armed with Carmen and Tess my colleague, having decided that his dogs were perhaps not quite fit enough for a population of this size. I took my turn to drive and so we travelled in my van: this decision was later to prove very decisive.

There was very little that we felt we could improve on regarding the way that we had tackled this farm the week before, and it was agreed that we would take the same route that had proved successful then.

Soon my two dogs were doing their thing and we got off to a good start. Weather conditions, however, were not as they had been the week before: the wind was strong and heavy, and increasingly frequent showers soon soaked us through. My colleague soon started complaining about the weather. Having originally played deaf to his grizzling, I later tried encouraging him with my worldly wisdom that weather like this never lasts long and it will soon clear up. We continued: the wind got stronger and the rain became persistent. Again he grizzled something about madness and stupidity; fortunately the wind was so strong I could not hear him clearly.

It was about this time that I realised we were seeing very few rabbits; in fact, we had crossed a couple of fields that held none. The wind increased further, the rain stung our faces as it was propelled into us at such force that at one point we had to stop and turn our backs to the wind as the stinging became unbearable. Trees could be heard crashing down. My friend was now begging for us to go home. No, I would not entertain this cowardly act: he could walk home if he wanted, but it was my van and we were carrying on. It had been a long time since we last saw a rabbit: they had clearly returned to the sanctuary of their buries. The rain turned to hail and unbelievably the wind got stronger still. I succumbed to the temptation of the van and we made our way to it.

Having arrived at the van not a word was spoken. The dogs jumped in and we climbed into the front; again my friend persisted with his unwanted opinion of the madness of what we had just done. I decided that he needed to be enlightened on the world of lamping. "The weather we are suffering tonight is nothing. I have been out in worse than this loads of times and furthermore, I have no problem with it at all." Silence fell, which soon developed into an uncomfortable silence. I put the radio on in an attempt to ease the tension and within seconds the tune being played was stopped and a newsflash was delivered to reveal that the West Country was currently being hit by the worst storm it had suffered in over sixty years: people were being advised not to go outside.

The timing of that was incredible: we both laughed and appreciated the moment, but we never lamped together again. I did contact him and apologise and offered a night out on some of my ground, but he declined, fearful of a repeat performance.

It was proving very fortunate that my preference was for lamping alone because slowly but surely I was burning any bridges that I had. I could never allow myself to give in to the weather: feeling cold or being wet was an occupational hazard and you just carried on. If the ground is frozen and the dogs may hurt their feet that is different: you stop. But short of a genuine governing reason such as that, nothing could be allowed to get in the way. Living this life there were no rules: you made them yourself. If you wanted an excuse not to do something you could very soon find one. I preferred to stay self-disciplined and not give in. I expected so much effort from the dogs I worked with: how could I then let them down and become the weak link in the side? That could not and would not happen.

When the moon was up, the dogs would recover and enjoy a much more leisurely couple of weeks. During this time I transferred from my nocturnal existence to a more recognised life of sleeping at night and being awake all day. During these periods I would use the ferrets to continue my rabbiting service, primarily visiting sites that were unsuitable for the dogs at night. I enjoyed this sport and never tired of the thrill of visiting heavily populated ground on a still frosty morning, when in the absence of wind you would hear all the action taking place below ground. Although I was a strong believer in using nets with the ferrets, I always liked to take at least one dog with me on these trips: there were not many days when the dog would not get at least one chance to add to the bag. Tess was my usual assistant on these occasions, having come along so often she now had a good understanding of what was going on, and having her there always proved very beneficial.

I now wanted Carmen to take part. I was interested to see how she would adapt to this form of rabbiting. There were nearly always moments when the dog would prove its worth for being included in the day: an unnetted hole, perhaps two rabbits bolting one directly behind the other from the same netted hole. The first, of course, would be caught; the second would be away were it not for the dog waiting to intercept it; sometimes rabbits will bolt before you have even finished netting up, and sometimes a rabbit will be disturbed, particularly on a bright morning, having decided to lie up in the undergrowth close by and enjoy feeling the winter sun on its back. These can be taken by the dog as they bolt back towards the bury that in other weather conditions they would have been living in safe underground. So it had proved time and time again to be well worthwhile having a dog present. But I wondered with her size whether Carmen would be quick enough off the mark to fill this role. Of the three dogs I had, Tina was the most physically suited to this role: her lightning-fast reflexes and seemingly instant top speed were really exactly what was required, but Tina did not enjoy lying on the ground on cold days waiting for netting up to be completed, and I always ended up feeling sorry for her. She had served me so well over the years: she deserved and had indeed earned this consideration, so unless it was a really nice day I spared her this unwanted duty.

Carmen knew the ferrets: she had been introduced to them as a puppy and they lived in a hutch right beside the kennel so she knew they were on our side. The first time Carmen came out, the benefits of all her basic obedience training really showed: I chose some nice, easy-to-do, small ground buries. Carmen was shown where to lie down and instructed to stay. I could see that she almost instinctively knew what we were doing: I guess the smell of rabbits in that area must have been strong and her being so smart she could just feel something was about to happen. As I carefully and very quietly moved around the bury placing a purse net (a net with draw cords that when the rabbit bolts the net closes around it in a 'purse' and is restrained by a peg pushed into the ground) on each hole, I occasionally glanced up to see what she was doing: she was watching me intently every time. I could see that she was not going to move until instructed: her 'stay' had been learnt so well.

Eventually all was ready. The ferret was deliberately placed on the ground away from any hole: this served several purposes, the most important of which was to re-enforce the fact to Carmen that the ferret was indeed on our side and not to be touched. Secondly it gave me the opportunity to go and crouch beside her and see her through this introduction.

Eventually the ferret, guided by its nose, disappeared below ground; not long after it went out of sight the rumbling beneath ground revealed that a rabbit was on the move. Carmen's head went to the side, her ears pricked up, and she stared at the ground from where the noise had come from. Suddenly it started again and this time it continued and we had our first bolt. The rabbit hit the net and Carmen stood up: a whispered 'no' and a forceful stay made it clear to her that her help was not required. I told her to stay again and got up to go and take care of the rabbit we had caught and reset the net. Before I had finished, a second had bolted into a different net: Carmen sprang up and moved towards it: 'stay' held her again. The second rabbit was dealt with before the ferret showed. Given how small the bury was, it was most unlikely that this particular ferret would leave a rabbit behind, but it was tried once more nevertheless. There was nothing more at home and soon the ferret was back out again. I left the ferret trotting around on the ground as they do with their backs arched up, and took the opportunity to praise Carmen. She had not been needed but had still behaved and done exactly what was required.

Later that day, having enjoyed a nice, steady morning, we went to another very similar-sized ground bury which was quite isolated in regard to its nearest neighbouring bury, and I deliberately tried to get Carmen a run. No nets were used of course and once again the ferret was placed on the ground, as opposed to in the entrance mouth of the hole. I did not go to Carmen this time, but watched her from a distance. I hoped we would be lucky and find something at home. Again it was not long before the rumbling underground could be heard. Carmen moved but didn't stand: she was in a type of crouch, very collie-like, staring intently at the area the noise was coming from. Suddenly the rabbit was away, and as Carmen began to chase, I detected a definite moment of hesitation as she set off. I felt sure that she had expected to once again not be needed, and then almost immediately after this initial thought realised that in fact she was. She caught her rabbit which for her at that particular location could not have been easier and brought it back and received much praise for her efforts: the hoped-for second or even third rabbits from this bury did not materialise. It soon became clear that there was only one at home, so our first ferreting trip ended in this very productive manner.

It had all gone really well: there was not really anything more that I could have hoped for on Carmen's first experience of ferreting. The question of whether she would be quick enough off the mark to really make the ferreting grade had neither been tested nor answered, and it was much too early to draw any conclusions of how she would adapt to this form of rabbiting. What I did already know, though, was that she would always be coming ferreting from now on because I just loved to have her with me. She was no trouble at all to have there, so if she made it as a ferreting dog that could be looked at as a bonus, as opposed to any necessity. Tess, who had served me so well and knew ferreting inside out, could not be relegated just because of Carmen's arrival on the scene: in future, ferreting trips would be the three of us.

Carmen and Tess after a day's ferreting. The fox was removed from a snare on the same farm.

Carmen did indeed take to ferreting and fully contributed to both the success and certainly the enjoyment of any ferreting day we took. The collie crouch that she displayed on our first ferreting trip turned into her normal stance when she was anticipating a bolt; she very quickly understood that it was not acceptable to touch a rabbit already caught in a net, although I always had the impression that she did not agree with that ruling; despite this, she never broke it. Carmen and Tess worked well as a pair. Each would take up their own vantage point as the ferret was entered, and each would respect the other when their services were needed, and when a catch was made whoever caught it, kept it: they did not need telling that, as they seemed to work that out for themselves, and they never once attempted for it to be any other way.

Another habit that Carmen developed which proved very useful when attempting to ferret large hedge buries that were really better suited to two or more people working together was that when the ferret showed, she would point her nose to the ground and seemed to look at the ferret from the top of her eyeball; it was a mysterious reaction but it was consistent and very helpful, because as long as I could see Carmen from where I was standing I would be certain of when the ferret had showed on her side. I could watch her watch it and tell exactly the moment that the ferret either had gone back underground or was in danger of wandering away. When the ferret went back down, the angle of her head would change and her normal expression would resume. This must have been something personal between her and the ferret because later in life working with the terriers this activity never provoked this same reaction.

Rarely I would use the long nets in conjunction with the ferrets – rarely because of where the majority of ferreting took place, not because I did not favour them. Their use in ferreting I felt to be much better suited, though not restricted to being used whilst doing open-ground buries, and those areas for me at least very often coincided with areas I preferred to leave for lamping. However, when occasion demanded that we use the long net (a long, slack net normally 50 or 100 yards long supported by 3-foot stakes 5 yards apart in which the rabbits become tangled), we did, and both Carmen and Tess knew how to behave around them. For the dogs this was, I am sure, a very frustrating method for us to use as the chances of escape for the rabbit were very restricted, so the need for the dogs' assistance was as a result uncommon.

Of course our job was to catch the rabbits so the last paragraph questions why we would not use that method at all times. The answer is that where there were large numbers of rabbits we would indeed consider the use of long nets, but again those were places more likely to be lamped. The smaller, more awkward places typical of where we would ferret did not always have enough rabbits to justify either the time it took to successfully set them, or the difficulty of carrying them to site whilst working alone.

Whilst the ferreting was enjoyable the lamping is where our most productive work took place, and as the number of lamping nights out together for Carmen and I increased, the opportunity for any weakness she may have to reveal itself multiplied. This never happened: she had it all. Routes that I had followed for years were extended as a result of Carmen's stamina and ability to catch so quickly, thus saving her energy and prolonging our nights. The land we worked had previously kept me going all season, but now, with numbers depleted due to our success, we were able to take on and look for more.

I recall going into the local town one Saturday morning through necessity, and walking along the main street three butchers whose businesses were all adjacent to each other had rabbits hanging along the top of their shop windows as they used to back in those days, still in the skins: side by side they covered the whole shop frontage, and one had them two deep. Every one had been caught by Carmen during that particular week. I stood and watched people look at them as they went by: one butcher came out and lifted one down using a stick, obviously in the process of making a sale. How many people would have believed where they had all come from? I had again through necessity also located a new group of additional butchers in other neighbouring towns to supply since Carmen's arrival: she had made such an impact.

One serious problem that I had to deal with was in areas where there was no drop-off point from where Carmen's catch could be collected by van later; I was really struggling. We worked a lot of cliff ground together: these areas were notorious for having to carry the catch and keep it with us. I could never bring myself to resist the chance of any run on any rabbit and would find myself landed in a serious predicament. Having fairly broad shoulders, my standard practice was to have my game bag [postman's bag] hanging on my left from my right shoulder, and my battery in a box hanging on my right side from my left shoulder. In my pocket I had 12 strings tied into appropriate loops. The first rabbit went into the bag, the second, by using a string, got braced with it and went over my right shoulder. The third into the now empty bag and so on, until all the strings were used up. The bag would then be filled; some of the braced rabbits would now be transferred to my left shoulder and I would be in trouble. The lead would then come into play, legging the rabbits and sliding them on. Previously I had always just about managed; now, thanks to Carmen's intervention, I feared it would be the death of me. Many nights I had to stop, unable to continue and carry a load to the nearest road. This could be quite some distance out of my way, but there was no alternative. By the time I returned to collect the second load I would normally be carrying quite a few more. It was a nice problem to have catching so many but this was hard to remember as my legs buckled under the weight, with rabbit fur stuck to my lips and the distinct aroma of rabbit urine for some reason following me around. I could not physically do it now, I am quite sure.

Throughout this happy period, unlike the other dogs, Carmen managed to stay practically injury-free. Tina, in particular, would be missing from the team at various times through the course of a season. Carmen would not: she had much thicker skin than the other two dogs, and this I believe – more than her beautiful rough coat – played a huge part in protecting her from lacerations. Her feet were strong and she never knocked a toe up in her whole life.

Throughout the lambing periods I had attended to my side of the bargain in protecting the various farmers' lambing fields for them by snaring, and had enjoyed considerable success. As usual, neighbouring farms or farming relatives in the next parish get to hear of the help available and more requests for help are soon forthcoming. Fox pelts at that time had a value and mine would be saved up frozen and then personally delivered in batches to the furrier. Fortunately for me, he was based not very far from where I lived, and so when the freezer was full and it became necessary I would take a trip down to see him.

If he reads this I know he will smile, as will anyone else who supplied him at that time. The pelts would be laid out on his extensive work surface: this one would be a good one that would go to the right in the £25 category, then immediately one would be found of lesser value that one went to the left in the £8 category. No matter how many pelts

I took down or how frequent my visits may be, my averaged-out price would be exactly the same.

However, despite these antics the furrier and I got on fine and on one visit our conversation turned to shooting which led to the revelation that he was starting a new, large-scale commercial pheasant shoot and would I like to work for him? Wow! It was instantly agreed, and what for me had been a lifelong dream had just come true in the most unexpected and sudden manner.

At my school careers interview years before, I had been asked if I knew what I wanted to do on leaving school. I knew exactly what I wanted to do, but on revealing that I wanted to be a gamekeeper I was instructed to forget that and be more realistic. This was the extent of the so-called careers advice I received; granted, I had never been a model pupil and so they were probably looking forward to getting rid of me, but even so when I think back that was not the right way to treat a youngster at that stage of his life. I wondered where that careers interviewer was now as I drove home wondering and imagining what the future may hold. Realising I was on the brink of getting an opportunity to fulfil my dream, I felt so fortunate and grateful for this extraordinary, unexpected chance.

By the time I had arrived home my excitement had been calmed by the knowledge that the life I had grown to love was about to change forever. There was no question that I was not going to jump at this opportunity, but equally there was no question I was going to so badly miss my current life. I had a two-month period in which to adjust and prepare for these changes.

Naturally my first thoughts were for my dogs. I decided after much heart-wrenching consideration that Tina, as she was getting old now, deserved her retirement: she had earned it and would stay with me for life. Tess was so skilled as a rabbiter and, being much younger than Tina, had so much left to give in this type of work that I felt that she would be better staying with a lamping colleague who I knew would give her an excellent home. This, though the hardest decision of all to make, would permit Tess to continue with the job in which she had so much left to offer.

Carmen was, as they say in these modern days, a no-brainer. Wherever I went she would always be with me. Compared with those decisions, everything else was easy to work out.

Having two months to prepare, I decided to make the most of them. I knew that it was most unlikely that I would ever live like this again. It had been an adventure and I had absolutely no regrets. I still often think back to this time and remember how many times I struggled to pay a bill or even buy essential food shopping before Carmen came along. Yet that period of my life had been one of my happiest: I would not change a thing.

For the next two months we continued our nightly excursions: whenever the conditions were right we took full advantage of every opportunity. As I walked at night I would think a lot and the two contrasting feelings of excitement for my new prospective career yet regret on losing the life I had grown to love created a strange mixture of emotion. As time progressed and the date grew nearer for me to start work (if that is what it was) more and more I became positive about this change. I recognised how fortunate I had been that this opening had come along and was determined that I would take full advantage and put every possible effort into it and repay the person who had given it to me in the best way possible.

Now that I would no longer be so reliant on the rabbits that we caught, I was desperate to answer a question that had nagged away at me for so long. How would Carmen cope being confronted by a strong winter hare? I had wanted to answer this for a long time but due to the already mentioned concerns, I had resisted the burning temptation to let her try. This was part of the reason why she had come into my kennel in the first place: after all, now I could see no reason not to try her out.

So early one January morning Carmen and I went out in search of a hare. We walked along the lane owned by a local market gardener who had always complained at the hares taking the middle out of his cauliflowers, seemingly whenever I saw him. At each gateway we stopped and scanned the field, finally in one of the larger fields which had been planted into winter wheat, a potential target was located. We entered the field and the hare squat flat: so far, so good. We walked towards it without aiming directly at it: if you walk directly towards a squat hare it will bolt and run away. We walked towards it, but our line would take us clearly wide of where he was squat. It was working a treat: the nearer we got, the flatter the hare went, so sure was he that we had not seen him. Carmen was off the lead but at heel. When we had reached what I felt was a fair distance, I turned and angled our line directly towards him. Almost immediately he got up and seemed to hit top speed. In an instant Carmen was away: she caught him up and the course was on. This was a strong winter hare out in a large field: this was the hare's domain and a good test for Carmen who, due to her winter's work, was supremely fit. She was soon up with him and he turned. She stayed with him and he turned again; suddenly she had him, far too quickly for what I had anticipated. I had genuinely thought she would find it far harder than that, especially given the field we were in. I must say in truth it proved an anticlimax: of course I was delighted that Carmen had caught her first hare, especially as the hare had all the odds in his favour, but she had found it far easier than I expected and I suppose I had been looking forward to watching her really tested. Carmen retrieved it to hand and just turned as if to look for another!

CHAPTER 3
KEEPERING

What had not perhaps fully occurred to me prior to our move was just what a change this was going to bring to Carmen's working life. She was no longer required to run rabbit after rabbit, night after night; instead, she could spend her whole day at work with me. Yes, we still went lamping: that was never going to stop, but now we went rabbiting for shorter periods, and should a fox appear in the lamp he would of course now take priority.

Carmen took to her new quarry as if she had hunted them her whole life. Her courage was there for all to see (although at that time, of course, nobody was) and the agility that she had mastered in her rabbiting years was now really helping her when dealing with this more formidable foe. Carmen's life opened up completely: she came with me everywhere: she travelled in the back of the truck. She actually caught a lot starting her run from the back of the truck. She now frequently took hares both in the day and of course at night.

Despite taking on these larger quarry species, she always remained soft-mouthed with her rabbits, thus proving my earlier concerns invalid: rabbits she retrieved undamaged live to hand for her whole life.

This was never better illustrated than one particular morning whilst we were dogging in straying pheasants, Carmen returned to me and I could immediately see there was something wrong or at least there appeared to be something wrong with her mouth. The closer she got the more I started to think that she may actually have something in her mouth, and by the time she got back to me, I was convinced this was the case. Offering her the palm of my hand, I was presented with a tiny rabbit so small that he fitted right into her mouth with it shut: he must have been taking one of his first looks at the big world outside his tunnel home and had got snapped up by a monster. Luckily for him, this monster carried rabbits with respect, seemingly no matter how small they may be and he was unceremoniously dropped into my hand. He was as slimy as slimy could be, but short of that none the worse for his ordeal.

I knew the bury nearest to where Carmen had appeared from and suspected that to have been the place she had found him. Arrival at this bury strengthened my suspicion, with the tiny little droppings scattered at the mouth of one particular hole. I dried him off with my shirt the best I could before reaching into the hole as far as I could and giving him another chance at life. So much for fox and hare making a dog hard-mouthed: if that truly is the case, nobody had told Carmen.

The shoot I had gone to work on was a new venture. The estate on which it was based had not previously explored the prospect of sustaining a large-scale commercial shoot before. As a result of this when we started working there I was one of five new keepers, of which none had any knowledge of the ground on which we worked. It was immediately apparent that there was a lot more ground, primarily forestry, included in the shoot lease than the shoot intended to utilise. This extensive block of forestry created a margin than ran down one side of the estate. Its far edge, 5-7 miles long, was our boundary with neighbouring farmers less than enthusiastic about permitting us to lamp their ground in order to control foxes. Many of them in fact were hunt followers known to actually feed foxes to encourage them onto their land. Gradually we developed a system that we felt was the best form of fox control available to us under the circumstances.

We were snaring and lamping where we could on what was effectively the centre and the northern edge of the estate as much and as often as possible, leaving the practically unchartered, forested southern edge until the spring when we would join forces and hunt for cubs together.

Being unfamiliar with the ground, the earths [dens] were unfamiliar to us as well, so in an attempt to combat this handicap we would form a line spread 8-10 trees apart and walk it up together. If anyone came across anything of interest, we would stop and try the terriers. This method proved productive and, whilst we accepted that it was far from ideal to have such a large area only temporarily and occasionally checked, in the absence of a better suggestion we persevered with this method.

Personally I saw it as if we had two shoot boundaries: one that we could cross when we were able or wanted to, and one that we could not. I enjoyed the days that we spent in there: Carmen absolutely loved it, always patrolling the line and always keeping alert and ready should her help be needed.

Working with the terriers was new to her but, having spent so much time ferreting, it was not really a surprise that she very quickly understood what we were doing – the similarities being so obvious –

and soon she was overseeing the project just as she had used to do when rabbits were our intended quarry.

Most of the success was gained through digging, but Carmen contributed on a regular basis, at times snatching older cubs as they attempted to bolt, trying to avoid the attention of the terriers. Occasionally we would get a vixen bolt which again Carmen would deal with very quickly, being constantly alert and always ready. Once or twice she caught foxes that we had inadvertently disturbed as we walked these thick plantations; these, though few, were a bonus and each one we caught removed another threat to the welfare of our future in-coming pheasant poults. Whenever we had located a family of cubs, any earth or bury nearby would be checked by the terriers to see if either or both of the parents were nearby. Finding the vixen at home with the cubs became less likely the older the cubs got, but we would regularly find

Carmen with her terrier mates displaying their catch of April 1992

the parents of the cubs, particularly the vixens, close by. Near enough for them to be able to easily access the cubs, but far enough away to get a break from the cubs keeping on: some of the wounds on the vixens' teats were so sore where the cubs had torn their mother whilst suckling.

The photo that accompanies this chapter was taken of catches made in April 92. The brushes were saved by a young lad who worked with me at the time, who insisted on saving them, much to my disapproval. Without insisting, I heavily recommended that he stop this pointless exercise, but by the end of the month which had been quite successful I found myself asking him, much to his delight, to set them up so that I could take a picture to remember this productive time by.

News of our foxing exploits travelled, and one evening I was contacted by a neighbouring farmer who said that he desperately needed help in his lambing field: he had lost a number of lambs and his own attempts of dealing with the culprit had proved unsuccessful. Although his farm did not border our estate, I said that I would be happy to try and help. He said that it was very important that his neighbouring farmers knew nothing of what was intended. Typical and not in any way totally unexpected, but when lambing was over I knew that the fox would not need to travel far to get in amongst our release pen sites, so helping him had potential benefits to ourselves as well.

I got to the farm at the agreed time and was invited in for a cup of tea where a rough description of the lie of the land was given. The disappointment on the farmer's face when he realised that I was completely unarmed and only intended to use a dog was not at all well concealed.

He said he had to come and see this, as he could not imagine how I thought I had any possible chance of success without a gun. What then followed was by far the shortest night's lamping I certainly have ever had and I would imagine most people have ever had.

We left his farmhouse and walked down the lane between two big sheds. On clearing the sheds as he had described we had a good view of the whole lambing field, and almost immediately we could see a fox. Whether it was *the* fox was impossible to say, but the ewes and lambs that were evenly spaced around it and seemingly calmly feeding did not suggest that he was causing them any undue concern, not at least at that particular moment anyway. Carmen was away clearing the fence with ease as she went. 'Get,' said the farmer as she jumped. 'Get,' said the farmer as Carmen raced across the field. The sheep scattered as she approached them, but she only had eyes for one thing and he was heading towards the far side of the field. As she caught up with him, he turned to our left. 'Get,' said the farmer, saving his biggest and grand finale 'Get' for when Carmen made contact and potentially solved his problem for him. He genuinely could not believe what he had just seen, nor could he stop saying 'Get'. But as far as he was concerned, our night started and finished there. No matter how much I tried to persuade him to allow us to continue, he was adamant that was it, job done, home time. I asked if he would mind if we carried on alone. No, he didn't want that to happen: it was perfectly clear that after one run and not even getting as far as entering a single field, our lamping trip was over.

To be fair to the farmer he was very complimentary towards Carmen and said he would never have believed what had just happened if he had not seen it for himself. So many people through the years were to share this sentiment: he even offered financial reward for our trouble which, as always, was declined.

I never heard from him or ever saw him again, so always assumed that the fox we caught may well (as it turned out) have been the right fox for him.

Before the pheasant poults were released into their woodland release pens we would habitually dog the pens out to ensure that nothing had inadvertently been shut in that could pose either a threat or a disturbance to the young birds. Any ground game would cause no end of disturbance to the young ground-roosting poults that first arrived; of course, a fox would prove catastrophic. Carmen loved this job: she worked out what was happening very quickly and would take up any prominent position she could find from where she was offered a good, clear view. She did not participate in the hunting up aspect of the project: whilst perfectly capable of doing so when alone, on these pack-handed occasions she preferred to allow the terriers and spaniels to do the hunting whilst she stood on guard. But how seriously she took her role, the level of concentration she showed, was frankly way beyond what was really needed, but that was her: give her a job to do and it would get done thoroughly. If something was in that pen she would deal with it. It was very unusual for anyone to spot something before she did. If there was anything in the pen – and of course at times there was: after all, these were massive pens – the first indication of its presence would be when she started to make her move. Whatever it may be was quickly dealt with and the pen was soon rendered safe to use for its intended purpose. My keepering colleagues would often ring to say they were clearing their own pens and ask if I would come over to assist. It appeared initially as if they would like my help. In reality I knew, that they knew, if I was there, Carmen would be there, and then the task would instantly become much simpler.

One morning a keeper friend from my home area visited to take a busman's holiday. We spent a lovely day together going around the estate looking at and discussing the drives which had been created, and the merits and failings of each and all the other related topics that this type of day leads you into. One of his observations was the large size of our release pens which somehow led us into talking about how Carmen performed when assisting with the final check of the pens before poults were released. This was a friend of long standing and he had known Carmen back in our pre-keepering days when she was my number one rabbiter: he was interested and pleased to hear how she had adapted.

The discussion progressed and ideas flowed: before long, we were examining the prospect of moving roe from the estate I was on to the one where he was based. They had no deer at all on his estate at that time, something that was of great regret to him, and he could sense that an opening was starting to develop that could suit and satisfy everyone's viewpoints.

The owner of the estate I was working frankly didn't care how the numbers were reduced, but reduced they must be and the sooner, the better. He had a great interest in the forestry operation and the high number of deer present were of constant concern to him and his forestry team. I must say that one recent Christmas I revisited this estate and enjoyed a walk some twenty-five years after I was last there and, although disappointingly there is no longer a shoot there, the standard of the forestry management is a credit to all his efforts. Areas that I remember as impenetrable bramble smothering young trees have been tended and well managed, and have now developed into stands of fine specimen trees.

Anyway, a plan was devised that would basically require me to repair my pens in the spring after catching up – catching the pheasants required for breeding purposes – had finished, but this time, unlike in normal years, I would leave part of a side wall open in the hope (although it was really inevitable) that roe would enter the pen which in this instance would be doubling as a trap. Pens would be checked regularly, and on being found to contain a suitable specimen, the side wall left open would immediately be closed. My counterpart in this project would do likewise in repairing his pens and have them ready for the intended new occupants. We both felt that this could work well, and if the deer were left quiet for two or three weeks in their new home to acclimatise before his gates were left open, there was every chance this project could succeed.

The only thing left was for him to approach his estate owner and tell him our plan: he loved the idea and couldn't wait to see deer gracing his land, and offered any financial help required. We needed no financial help of course, but I guess in his world of finance, money is the answer to so many things that the idea that someone could actually do something for the love of doing it and not expect reward was unthinkable.

Anyway, what had originally hatched as a madcap idea was now a full-blown plan, and the one fundamental part was to be played by Carmen. She had become so proficient at dealing with roe by now that there was little chance that she would let us down. She, we hoped, would hold the deer just long enough for us to get there and secure them and then they would be transported to their new home. The alternative for them would have been to be destroyed, so whilst I am sure capture caused them a degree of stress, the eventual outcome would at least offer them a second chance at life. Everyone would come out a winner. The reason the release pens were required, as opposed to just going out and catching any roe, was that when suitable targets had taken up residence in the release pens they could happily live enclosed in these pens until it was convenient to move them, and only suitable targets would necessitate the long journey required for collection: there was a considerable distance between the two estates.

In a very short space of time we had three roe living in two different pens, the pens were closed, phone calls were made and before you knew it we had reconvened onsite. The two of us discussed tactics so that we each knew our respective roles. We decided to first go to the pen holding the single specimen, a buck; he was not a trophy but he was a good example of his species and looked to be on the up, not going back. Eventually when we felt we were in position and ready, Carmen was allowed to go forward. She disappeared from my sight, but shortly after the crashing sound of breaking twigs and branches revealed that she had found our deer shortly after we could hear that she had made contact and we rushed to both her and the buck's aid. When we arrived she had her deer down and well under control. We relieved her of her catch and examined him for injury. Short of a small graze on his shoulder, which may or may not have been there already, he was in perfect condition. We sprayed his shoulder with wound spray gifted by the estate shepherd, just in case it could become infected, and placed him into a large sack ready for his journey. This was easy. The other roe were treated in the same fashion, and very quickly all three were ready for their journey. Carmen, it seemed, as always had excelled and had played her part perfectly: any slight reservations we had about our chosen method of capture proved unfounded and all had gone far better then we could have hoped for. The use of nets had initially been discussed but the unpredictable location of where exactly to set them had made us certain that Carmen would do the job far more quickly and far more efficiently; this had certainly proved to be the case. That spring we repeated this project twice more, each time efficiently securing our targets without injury and the release at the other end was reported to have gone equally well.

Perhaps, predictably, and undoubtedly encouraged by our success with roe, our discussions turned to the fallow – after all, what could go wrong? Well, it turned out, quite a lot: a group of about twelve took up residence in one of our larger pens.

Together we entered this pen full of confidence: our usual tried and proven method was again expected to take place. Five minutes later saw us standing looking at a decimated release pen with snapped posts and stretched, distorted mesh. This spectacle brought us quickly to our senses and we realised we had undoubtedly taken this project one step too far.

Years later, I now once again live in the area of the release site estate. Now roe are extremely widespread: of course not all will originate from our reintroduction programme of the early 1990s. Roe have become far more abundant throughout the region, but whenever I see any on or near that estate I wonder if in their distant ancestry any of our deer are represented. I hope so and like to think so.

At home the next landmark stage of our calendar year would be the arrival of the combine harvester on the estate. I would always try and be present as the combine approached the last few acres of each field, knowing that it could well present an opportunity to account for a fox or two. Initially I used to stand with Carmen whilst we watched the combine's progress but she quickly worked out what was going on and how this could work to her benefit. When she started leaving me as the combine came out of the standing crop to turn around, I realised that I was basically redundant: she would already be on her way to the other end of the field where once again she would take up her guard. At this stage in those seemingly pre-health and safety days, I started to ride on the combine. Standing armed with a shotgun on the platform gave me a fantastic view of all that was happening, and I used to look to the other end of the field at Carmen and be so proud of how she had adapted to our new way of life.

Hares were both plentiful and unwanted in such numbers on the estate by the farm manager and Carmen took many as they broke out from the standing crop. Sometimes she would have one whilst the combine still had a way to go to the end of its cutting strip. She would come towards the combine and the driver would allow me off to enable her to deliver her catch. All these catches were shared between the tractor drivers on duty, the combine driver and any other estate personnel that happened by at the right time. They loved it: entertainment to brighten their otherwise tedious day, in addition to a nice supper to take home. It was a win-win for them. Quickly she had became a bit of a celebrity on the estate. As the combine started to reach the last bit of each field, tractors that were loaded and ready to return to the farm would start to build up in numbers reluctant to leave the field waiting for the grand finale.

Occasionally there would indeed be a fox in the crop caught out in its rapidly diminishing sanctuary. The combine driver would sound the horn to encourage the fox to keep moving forwards: everyone present would know exactly what this meant and Carmen's stance would became even more intense, as impossible as that may have initially appeared to be. The fox would be moving forward and whilst watching it from my elevated position unable to shoot due to the close proximity of all those around, my concern would be that it would double back and somehow sneak out. When eventually it bolted I had no concerns at all: all my worries completely, instantly disappeared. I trusted her completely and knew she would deal with it. Carmen never once missed a fox from in front of the combine: they were dealt with very quickly. The only time one did manage to momentarily delay the inevitable was when he dived into a thick row of neighbouring cut straw and failed as per normal to reappear: a good move on his part, to be fair, but it didn't fool Carmen for long. He was quickly taken as he reappeared heading back towards the standing crop from where he had just left.

On a shoot day whilst Carmen completely understood that the pheasants were not to be touched, should a rabbit, hare, fox or deer show, then she took over. Our beaters never once complained at the regular supply of venison this provided, nor did the forester ever complain about the beaters going through his young trees, knowing full well that, due to Carmen's prowess, he stood to gain far more from our activities than he ever stood to lose. Paying guns delighted in the spectacle of her coursing should they be afforded a distant glimpse of what was happening, and after any incident in the day that would without exception inevitably become the topic around the dinner table that evening.

I recall on one drive that we used to call 'Sherwood', a fox bolted from the top of the wood, heading in what ordinarily without Carmen's presence would have been a very good choice of direction in which to run, soon realising he had no chance of making the distant cover for which he was heading. He took emergency action and returned to the wood that he had just appeared from; this time, however, his path took him into the wood behind the line of beaters, as opposed to being in front of them as he had previously been. My view of the incident ended with Carmen entering the wood hot on his trail, but still with a lot to do. I remember thinking, maybe but probably not. She was gone for long enough to raise suspicion that she may have made contact but as none of the beaters had any light to throw on the matter, by the end of the drive it was a growing assumption that she had probably not been successful this time.

The pheasant drive itself, though, had been a success and in good spirit we started to walk towards our tractor and trailer collection point, knowing that Carmen would catch up with us shortly as she had done on numerous occasions before: she knew exactly where we would be. My employer who was hosting the day then came over the radio to say that guns number seven and eight, who were in an unusually isolated spot on Sherwood, had rejoined the rest of the guns at the bridge meeting point, telling the tale of a dog catching a fox, seemingly killing it, and then carrying it off. "I wonder who that could have been?" he remarked, knowing full well who that would be. His report, heard by most of the group of beaters present, instinctively encouraged several, including myself, to turn back to look towards Sherwood, and there heading our way was Carmen with her catch. The inquest at the end of the day revealed – thanks in no small part to numbers seven and eight – exactly what had taken place.

Carmen had a strange never-to-be-explained view that some of the foxes she caught, but not all, should be retrieved. How she selected those that should from those that should not I could never work out. One thing for sure was that they were not selected by the ease of the task. Given that we now knew what had happened and from where she had brought this fox, that was an extraordinarily difficult retrieve. I went out to her and relieved her of her catch and quietly gave her what I knew she still loved, praise.

On another occasion, having just arrived at the Shoot Lodge to see the guns at the end of the shoot day, an estate worker came over the walkie-talkie radio, which as the estate demanded was constantly on my belt. He reported that he had just removed a silage bale from a pile of about 40 bales stored behind one of the farm buildings at the home farm, and that he had disturbed a fox which had bolted out and subsequently gone back and returned into the same pile. The guns all over hearing this report, listened with interest, asked what was going to be my next step. I told them that I would be going home to get a terrier and try to get him out. Could they come? Yes, of course if you really want to, but you will have to keep quiet and out of the way. Half an hour later saw us arrive at the bales. Three tractor drivers, having heard the news, had now also assembled to spectate. They knew exactly what to expect: they had all seen Carmen in action at harvest time working in front of the combine. All of them had enjoyed a roast hare supper thanks to this dog: now they just wanted to watch.

The terrier quickly found and surprisingly, despite my unspoken reservations the fox readily bolted, the direction he then took offered everyone a first-class view as Carmen dealt with him very quickly and efficiently. The guns talked of nothing else: on the shoot we had just put on a 400-bird day with a very high standard of shooting yet the highlight of the day had been Carmen taking what for her was a very simple opportunity at a fox. Of course, the guns, not having seen anything like that before, could not appreciate that this was indeed a simple opportunity for a dog like her. I was certainly not going to steal her glory by telling them. The tips were good that night and I am sure Carmen's exploits had contributed to the guns' generosity. I wonder if that tale ever still gets told around a shoot table. I doubt whether any of those guns present that evening ever saw that type of thing happen again: these days with social media as it is, it would have no doubt been flashed around the country as quickly as it happened, but back then in those much happier times it was reserved for those who were present alone.

As well as formal driven days, shooting this particular shoot offered much smaller and very informal walked-up shooting (rough shooting where the guns walk as opposed to formal where the guns stand at predetermined spots indicated by pegs in the ground, with birds to be presented over these spots/pegs by a controlled team of beaters). On these days we would take advantage of the opportunity of basically dogging in with anything from one to four paying guests accompanying us and enjoying some mixed bag rough shooting at the same time. I enjoyed these days with the right guests who were true sportsmen: they were really enjoyable.

CARMEN

My employer advised me that there was one American individual who would like just a morning's walked-up shooting, a single gun who may or may not be accompanied by his non-shooting wife for company.

There was nothing particularly unusual about that: myself and two trainees met up to greet him. As soon as we met him there was a strong suspicion that this was not going to be a normal morning.

He had a really strong American accent and was full of it: his wife or servant, depending on how you viewed their relationship, was quite clearly pregnant. He looked, dressed and sounded just like Boss Hogg from *The Dukes of Hazzard*.

Anyway, routine formalities started their visit to the shoot with a welcome speech and a reminder of safety being of paramount importance at all times. That was breath wasted that I will one day need.

Before we set off I questioned whether the lady may like to stay in the shoot lodge where there was heat, a kettle and magazines that she could enjoy in front of a bay window which offered a panoramic view of the valley below. "No, Guy, she is coming with us." "My name is Phil, sir." "Oh yeah. OK, Guy." I caught the eye of his wife who did not have to say a word: her face said so much with a mixture of both apology and embarrassment.

We progressed to a goyle that always held pheasants, but more importantly on this particular day on one side of which had comfortable walking with the lady in mind. Soon the spaniels were finding birds for Boss Hogg to miss. Every excuse that could possibly be found was found. The dogs, his gun, the cartridges, the ground – at one point he even questioned what Carmen's problem was. "What's wrong with that dog, Guy? Why does it not do anything?" It was not even worth trying to explain.

Again I caught his wife looking in my direction: she was paying a high price for her life of luxury, and I hope she felt it was a good deal.

A snipe unexpectedly flushed and Boss Hogg wasted another two cartridges. "Why don't we see more of them, Guy?" "Because we are in the wrong habitat, sir." "Let's go get more of them, Guy!" Going snipe shooting with someone who could not shoot and had a pregnant wife at heel did not seem anything like in my opinion a good idea. Trying to explain that his wife would not manage the marsh comfortably was wasting more breath because Boss Hogg was intent on that was where we were heading.

We arrived at the marsh. The two trainees were absolutely loving every minute of it. "Perhaps your wife would like to wait here and watch, sir?" "No, Guy, she is coming with us." She had no say in the matter. Despite my advice, he insisted that this 'mighty fine woman' came with us. Predictably it was more than she could manage. Finally Boss Hogg decided in the most inappropriate spot possible that she could stay on a bank and wait for us. I tried to explain that this was potentially the worst possible place for her to stay, as it was going to place a severe restriction on where he could safely shoot. "If the lady wants to stay, she is staying, Guy." "My name is Phil, sir!" "Yeah, you told me!"

"OK, if she stays there you can only shoot forward, sir." "No problem, Guy." We walked on. As I glanced back I saw her perched on a mound and settled on her coat; we still had nothing at all in the bag. Again Boss Hogg enquired, "What's wrong with that dog?" indicating towards Carmen. "There is absolutely nothing wrong with this dog, sir." I saw the trainees glance at each other and smile. Suddenly a snipe flushed behind us: Boss Hogg fired both barrels and his wife rolled off her perch and disappeared from view. I genuinely thought Boss Hogg had shot his wife. After what seemed a lot longer than it probably was she reappeared and waved to signal all was well. Even the trainees did not laugh this time, equally shocked. Both spaniels were called into heel as we left the marsh, and I prayed that no more snipe were seen.

We collected Mrs Hogg and started to make our way up the side of a rough piece of ground. One of the spaniels went on point, staring intently at a clump of rough grass and reed. "Right, come and stand here, sir, there is definitely something here, get yourself comfortable and ready." Boss Hogg took up his position, and everyone else got in behind: there was nothing that could go wrong. "Are you ready, sir?" A whispered "Yeah, Guy." An accidental snort from a trainee trying not to laugh broke the silence. The spaniel was sent to flush and a hare bolted from its seat. Bang, the first barrel went off visibly in the wrong direction. Bang, the second went off whilst the gun was pointing skywards as a result of the recoil from the first. Carmen sprung into action and was in hot pursuit. "What's that dog doing, Guy?" "She is trying to retrieve it for you, sir." "Why doesn't she just grab it, Guy?" The fact that Carmen was doing her level best on a strong winter hare and was a genuine sight to behold was completely wasted on this idiot. Carmen turned her hare several times, once or twice getting groans from the trainees who were willing her on. They had seen her catch plenty but, like me, they really hoped that she would catch {retrieve!} this one for us. The hare went under the gate and Carmen went over and both were gone from view. Boss Hogg turned around and said, "You should have sent one of them good dogs, Guy!" referring to the two spaniels which had provided him with game to miss all morning. Clearly considering that a spaniel would easily be capable of outrunning a strong winter hare, it was not even worth a reply.

Suddenly a trainee said, "She has got it." Carmen was back in our field and returning with her catch. Boss Hogg in his delight threw his gun down and set off towards Carmen as fast as he could travel in wellies that clearly didn't fit and somehow managed to come over his knees. As he approached her she looked at him sideways and ran around him and left him in her wake. She delivered the hare which I then presented to Boss Hogg on his out-of-breath arrival back to where we were standing. "I am telling you, Guy that is the biggest darn rabbit I ever did see." the trainees and I all laughed aloud. There was no point in worrying about etiquette anymore: this idiot was so much that I dislike about the human race – who cared what he thought of us?

An 800-acre block of forestry on this estate had been leased to the Forestry Commission: they had their own ranger who looked after the deer and squirrel control in this area on their behalf. Everything that Boss Hogg was this ranger was not: our jobs pushed us together but in no time at all it became evident that we had a common interest in all wildlife-related topics, from counting nightjars, which I loved to help with, to finding the first set of red deer twins either of us had ever seen. Top of the list for both of us, however, was rabbiting, it was so nice to find someone else with a strong passion for what he did. On his periodic visits to the estate we spent hours, I am sure our employers (had they known) might have said wasted hours discussing and sharing theories, opinions and experiences on this shared interest.

His speciality was long netting, something that whilst I had spent plenty of time long netting rabbits in comparison to him, I was very much a novice.

His interest in rabbiting had led to him becoming interested in lurchers, and he was very keen to make this our topic of conversation whenever the chance presented itself.

I had absolutely no problem with that at all.

Predictably, a night out with Carmen was soon arranged, and I must say that this was one rare occasion when I was quite happy to have company. The ranger had access to some very suitable lamping ground with a strong population of rabbits and, as a result, we had a great night out with Carmen running well and securing a bag in excess of what had been expected. The ranger was suitably impressed and his thoughts about getting his own dog were, I believe, heavily influenced that night.

We had got to be very friendly and I thought it was great that he would be getting his own dog. I felt certain that, being the type of chap that he was, he would do very well with it. However, it was very difficult to try and find the right words to explain that not all lurchers are Carmen's. What he had just seen performed was a result of a combination of so many contributory things: Carmen's experience, her drive and mentality, her natural ability, to name just a few. I tried to explain how you could not just go and obtain that without being extremely lucky as I had been, and even then having received such good fortune lurchers needed to be trained properly and given the opportunity to fulfil whatever potential they may have.

It is so easy to say and yet so few people are actually able to offer this level of opportunity to their dogs.

For Carmen this was life, she absolutely loved what she did and she did it on a daily basis: she had matured into an exceptional dog. Was this because of what cross she was? Did anyone honestly know what cross she was? Or could this just be a genuine dog whose heart was completely in what she did, living in circumstances that provided her with the opportunity to fulfil her potential to the full. Amongst all these uncertainties one thing for certain was that I couldn't care less what cross she was; she had a wealth of experience in all ground game and had proved herself to be capable of quickly adapting to any new discipline presented to her, and I thought the absolute world of her.

Occasionally on favourable nights I would take Carmen out alone lamping, hoping to just see rabbits. Should that happen we could try to step back in time and for at least a short while try to relive our previous life together, but it just wasn't the same anymore; it wasn't necessarily worse, just not the same. I now had a good regular wage, free accommodation, my bills were paid - even my dog food was provided. An escaping rabbit now was no longer the financial disaster it once was: an escaping rabbit was not by any means common, but when inevitably it happened it failed to have anything like the disappointing impact it would have had two years previously.

Both of our lives would never be the same again. I felt sure that, given the choice, Carmen would have chosen the life she now had. Personally I was living a dream yet still yearned for the life that I strangely knew I didn't want to go back to.

The bond between Carmen and myself had now become so strong: I loved constantly having her with me and I suspected she felt the same, never settling down to rest on any day away from wherever I was. Whilst she took her own place in whatever we were doing, I would often glance at her to check where she was and would often find her looking my way at the same time, doing her own checking. When that happened it never failed to make me feel special and so privileged. Sometimes I would pause and watch her and remember the life-threatening journey that I embarked on to get her as a pup; I would remember the questions placed on my sanity by those who thought they knew better at contemplating such a journey in that particular mode of transport just for a dog. How wrong they had been. Carmen had never been just a dog.

On the occasions when she caught something whilst we were in the company of others, there was only ever one person who was going to be presented with it. Several people at various times thought it would be funny to relieve her of her catch, depriving me of my privilege of deciding whose turn it would be to have this bonus, only to be thwarted by her moving away from them and refusing to let anyone else have it. It was always treated as a joke, particularly amongst the beaters, but personally inside (though never revealed) it meant the world to me. We had come a long way together and both thought the world of each other.

Sometimes at night when the wind was blowing, I would hear her quietly whine in her kennel which was right outside my bedroom. The rain would beat against the window and I felt sure she was thinking the same as I was. The rabbits would be squatting tonight. But I would have to be up for feeding at first light, so we both slept in the warm and dry, whilst we both wished to be out in the cold and wet.

Carmen had developed, I believe, not only as a result of her attitude and clear natural ability in what she did. She was now working almost exclusively on one piece of ground: granted, it was a large piece of ground but it was her domain, she knew her way around. This was never demonstrated more clearly than early one morning when I was marking out ground that I hoped in the future I would be granted permission to plant into cover crop. I had discussed my plans with the estate manager who was not against the idea, but who asked me to mark it out so he could see exactly how big an area I intended to use.

So this is what I was doing this particular morning, armed with white pegs and a lump hammer, when the crack of a breaking branch from within the wood stopped me in midstride: that was something big. I looked to see where Carmen was: she was lower in the field then me, but closer to the wood. She was the first of us to move, having been stopped in her stride simultaneously by the same unmistakable sound. She ran uphill, cleared the stock fence at the top of the hill that separated the field that we were in from the bigger field that ran along the top of both our field and the wood. At the opposite end of the wood there was another gate that permitted access into another lower field. That end of the wood the far end as far as I was concerned was much narrower and she knew it: she had recognised that whatever it was would be moving away from us and proceeded to try and get to the other end first, or at least that's the way I read what was happening. She went out of my sight and all I could do was to get to the top fence – the one she had just cleared – and see if I could see anything from there. Nothing, all quiet. Suddenly there was a disturbance in the wood. Almost as soon as I heard it, the sound increased: whatever was making this noise was coming back my way and seemingly intent on breaking every twig and branch it passed. She must have either cut it off or gone to the far end of the wood and come back in from the opposite end. I was subconsciously trying to piece it together when the most fantastic melanistic {dark-coloured} fallow buck jumped over the hedge out of the wood right in front of me: what a sight. He was startled to see me and instantly turned to run down towards the bottom of the valley. I watched him set off and start his descent. Carmen then appeared over the same hedge in obvious pursuit: she was a good-sized bitch, but she looked so small behind him. I thought: no way.

The buck reached the six-strand wire fence that surrounded a strip of poplars in the bottom of the valley and cleared it with ease. Carmen copied him without breaking stride; they both then cleared with one leap the stream that ran through the middle of this plantation. The buck, several seconds in front of his pursuer, then ran uphill and under the young spruce on the other side of the valley and out of my view. Again I thought: no way. I followed the progress by sound alone as they went up through the spruce cover, seemingly intent on continuing to break every possible twig and branch on their way. As the distance between us grew, the noise diminished and I could only just still make it out when the unmistakable sound rang out: she had introduced herself and made contact. I would love to say I sprung into action at that moment, but, armed with only a hammer and on the wrong side of a stream that I knew I couldn't cross, that would be an incredibly inaccurate description of my reaction.

There was a bridge that the pickers-up used further down the valley. I made for that whilst still being able to hear where they were under the spruce cover. I crossed the bridge and ran up to a track that separated the spruce from the poplar. I became aware that there was no more sound: there was nothing to guide me in to her assistance. In fact, I was making so much noise myself I had to keep stopping like a blackbird hunting worms to see if I could detect any clues as to exactly where they were: there was nothing.

I knew roughly how far up in the wood they were when they came together, so decided to get to roughly that mark and then try to take it from there. This I did and eventually found her with the biggest buck I had ever seen. She was exhausted but that was not anything like as surprising to me as to what she had just accomplished. He was already dispatched, so I started to drag him down to the track. This then immediately presented the next problem, which was eventually overcome by means of a combination of winch and quad.

This run, as much as any, illustrated how her natural ability, combined with her intimate knowledge of the ground she worked, tipped the scales in her favour time and time again to contribute to her amazing success.

The trophy head of this buck remained on the side of Carmen's kennel for quite some time before a site inspection from a college tutor to see how one of our gamekeeping trainees was doing noticed it hanging there. He admired it and hinted how nice it would look hanging in the communal area that they were in the process of doing up for the keepering students at Bicton College.

I allowed him to take it as I thought that was a nicer place for it to be where it could be enjoyed by many more people: whether it is still there I know not, but if anybody reads this and has seen it that is where it came from. I would love to one day have it back?

One of our regular beaters had been asking for quite a time if I would take him out with Carmen at night. I always liked to try and repay the beaters in any way that I could, but this was really encroaching on our private time. Pigeon shooting in the spring, a joint of venison, a brace of birds at the end of the day – all the things that beaters enjoyed I was more than happy to offer in reward for their important shoot-day assistance.

Coming out with Carmen and me, though, was overstepping the mark – at least I thought it to be. I decided that if I just kept saying that it would happen one night he would eventually tire of asking and give up. He didn't.

Finally I was the one who relented and agreed that he could come out with us. The estate manager had expressed a concern at a relatively small number of rabbits that were starting to damage a recently planted field of Lucerne, and asked if the next time I was out I could go and take a look. As luck would have it, the night we went out the wind was blowing and it was warm and dry: a comfortable night to be out in. We entered the Lucerne field at the bottom end because all the buries were in either that hedge or the small rough area below it, so it was well known that this would be the direction in which the rabbits would go when disturbed. My persistent beater had been thoroughly briefed and would have no excuse if he got in our way. He was a keen ferreter but had never been lamping or, of course, seen a lurcher run at night before.

Our tactic would be simple: he would keep out of the way, Carmen would catch rabbits, she would give them to me, and I would then give them to him. He, a self-proclaimed expert at dispatching rabbits, would then do what he had to, and together we would progress.

As we entered the field I noticed that a tractor had been driven along just inside the hedge and parallel with the hedge the ground had clearly been soft at the time, and in doing so the tractor had created a rut not overly deep, but nevertheless there was a noticeable depression in the ground.

Our first rabbit was spotted very close by and was immediately taken out of its squat: Carmen delivered her catch I gave our friend his first victim. A second rabbit was already bolting for home. Carmen was away again: the rabbit reached the rut and tripped itself up, and Carmen was on her way back with number two. During her second run I had noticed a third rabbit also squat close by, so telling our mate to hurry up and take the second catch, Carmen was already on her way out for number three. Number three also fell to the rut-Carmen combination, and our friend was mumbling something. Rabbits four and five quickly followed before our 'helper' (!!) called a halt to proceedings.

When I turned around he had not had time to dispatch any of our catches and was struggling to contain his cargo with just about every part of his buckled body all at the same time.

It was farcical sight, one in which, with the absence of any sympathy whatsoever, I decided to take full advantage of and make him feel as bad about his inadequacies as I possibly could. "What's the matter with you? What are you doing? I thought you said you had been rabbiting before? Come on, you are holding us up." He apologised repeatedly all night long and also by phone the following morning, and never asked to come out again.

On the next shoot day our beaters were treated by him to a hugely exaggerated tale of how Carmen could catch rabbits faster than he could dispatch them: her reputation continued to grow and grow.

What perhaps I ought to have mentioned to him and his captive audience was that the only reason this happened in this way was the effect that the recently made tractor rut had in catching the rabbits out and tripping them up. Carmen did her bit, but for her it was simplicity itself. Our friend, however, had not noticed this contributing detail, struggling as he was not to lose our catch. Perhaps now 24 years after the event is a good time to come clean? Or perhaps I should leave it a bit longer?

One evening just as it was getting dark, the estate manager knocked on the door. He was visibly uncomfortable at needing to ask for help. Shoot/estate relations were not strong, as having a large-scale commercial shoot on its land had proved to have a much bigger impact than the landowners had anticipated and, as a result, the lease was not to be renewed. So we were seeing out our time, leading to an inevitable end.

The estate manager had a foreign stalking client who had just wounded a fallow deer that had been lost in a larch plantation near where we lived and he wondered whether 'that dog of yours' might find it.

I ignored the opportunity of asking what they were thinking of shooting at that time of night, as this was clearly not going to help the now stricken animal.

I did think it revealing, however, that he had asked for the help of 'that dog of yours'. I had a kennel of eight dogs at the time, but we both knew which one he meant.

Carmen had never attempted this before and I toyed with the idea of fixing a collar with a long piece of baler cord that was already on a spool which we used to obtain straight lines whilst building our release pens; somehow that did not seem to be the way to go. Deciding instead to play to our strengths, we set off with just our lamp.

So, having handed the estate manager one of our shoot-day radios, and taking a second myself, I told him to wait with his guest and I would give him a shout if we were successful.

We were directed to the location where the fallow had been standing when the shot had been fired and told that it had been seen to go down to the stream across to the other side and then up into the larches from where it had become unsighted again.

I encouraged Carmen to go forward. She unsurprisingly picked up the scent, given how soon we were there after the incident had happened, and that we knew exactly where the animal had been standing. That at least was expected. She led me down to the stream. I could just make out her silhouette in the failing light but remained reluctant to use the lamp unless I really had to, preferring instead the semi-darkness and silhouettes. Carmen reached the stream as expected but then started to go up the side of the very small, shallow stream, as opposed to crossing it into the larches as we had been instructed.

The estate manager, still able to see us, called out that it went up into the larches above us. Carmen did not seem to think so and was on the brink of going out of sight. I did not reply to the estate manager, preferring to trust Carmen's nose. Although we had never done this before I could not imagine her not being able to follow a scent this fresh.

I told Carmen to stay and momentarily remembered all the training sessions it took her as a stubborn pup intent on never staying to obey this command. Tonight she did it instantly and I hurried to catch up with her before asking her to go on again. As I reached her it had become darker, as we were now under the shadow of the larch wood above us. I decided to put the light on and followed Carmen further up the stream. The estate manager, due to the light being on, was now able to see exactly where we were and called out again that we were looking in the wrong place. I was just grateful that he had not had the sense to use the radio I had given him.

I told Carmen to stay again as she prepared to go out of sight for a second time around a corner onto the track that separated the larch from the much older spruce. As I used the light to pick my path I could see a blood trail and it was thick, dark blood: I felt certain now that we would indeed find the deer. I caught up with her again and did not need to tell her to go on again as, by using the lamp, I could see our fallow further down the track lying on the bank that led up into the spruce. It was quite dead, and the shot did not appear to have been that badly placed. Nevertheless, they should not have taken it in my opinion. However, I was not going to say anything and was glad that the deer had not suffered the indignity of not being recovered.

I radioed the manager and recommended that he return to his vehicle and drive around the valley so that he could get vehicular access to the track we were on.

Carmen stood on the bank quietly waiting for what came next, not realising that we had achieved all we had set out to do. "Good girl, Carmen." I so rarely used her name it was a wonder that she remembered it at all. Her tail wagged and she came over and pushed into my leg: she still loved praise. I had enjoyed that exercise and had never even considered not trusting her when she was not following the pattern of what we had been told had happened. The sound of a truck engine could be heard approaching so I dragged the deer further up the bank completely clear of the track. The headlights could now be seen and soon we were being lamped ourselves: we stepped off the track as the vehicle approached. All the expected excuses of how sure they had been that the deer had gone up into the larch replaced the previous claim that it had definitely been seen to do exactly that. Anyway, whatever had happened, they had their deer. More importantly, the deer had not suffered. I declined the offer of a lift home, preferring instead to enjoy a walk through the wood with Carmen, knowing that this would be one of the last times that we would be in this area as my intention was to start applying for any gamekeeping vacancies that arose elsewhere.

As I walked along the track I thought about when my daughter was little more than a baby and how we would walk along here on a Sunday afternoon. I would hold Lynsey on Carmen's back, Carmen being her pony for the afternoon. Carmen had been so loving to my children, yet anyone who saw her at work when a fox was being dealt with would have never believed it possible. I admired Carmen so much.

I also remembered when we were seeing out our last season as full-time rabbiters together, wondering how Carmen might adapt to our new life of gamekeeping. Never once had I ever considered that she would turn into the all-round versatile dog that she now was. Now on this evening, with her having been the unsung hero once again, I wondered what or where would be next. Wherever I went and ended up, one thing that was certain was that she would be right there with me.

Shortly after we arrived home a truck could be heard coming down the lane. The estate manager, having said his farewells to his stalking friend, had come over to say thank you.

Our relationship had become quite strained in recent times, but he had recognised that we had helped him out and he appreciated it. I was grateful for this acknowledgement and did not feel it necessary to reveal that my concerns had been more for the deer than for him.

He commented on Carmen's tracking ability and asked if there was anything that she couldn't do. I told him that in my eyes she couldn't do any wrong and we both smiled. He offered his hand and I shook it.

CHAPTER 4
SCOTLAND

Having taken the decision to seek a new job and a new challenge, I applied for most of the gamekeeping jobs that were advertised. I was very fortunate that, armed with a glowing reference from my previous employer with whom I had shared a very strong working relationship, I was invited to attend several interviews for these various gamekeeping positions. From these invitations I had selected two that I felt sounded to be the type of position I was searching for. The first was in Hampshire; the second was at the other end of Britain in Scotland.

The interview in Hampshire took place first, it was supposed to be a two-stage interview where the selected six applicants chosen for the first round of interviews in day one were reduced to two, who would then be asked to come back for a more in-depth interview on the eventual second day.

I believe more perhaps because of the other applicants' unsuitability than any particular thing that had happened in my very brief initial interview, the proposed second interview was cancelled and I was offered the job. Nevertheless, given that I had only been afforded a brief 30-minute allotted time, I arranged to visit the estate again before committing to this offer. This has very little to do with Carmen of course, other than that the second, more in-depth conversation revealed that this estate had suffered a tremendous amount of poaching by lurchermen due to the large population of brown hares it held, and how the estate was dealing with this problem was both of interest and also became relevant in comparing contrasting outlooks of other landowners at a later date.

What this particular Hampshire estate had done was to catch a locally well-known group of poacher's red-handed hare coursing with their lurchers. However, instead of the normal procedure of involving the police which, in turn, would almost certainly lead to some form of tit-for-tat revenge, they offered a deal. The estate would permit them to have the hare-coursing rights across the whole estate on the condition that they always let the head keeper know when they were coming; they must also accept that at this time the keeper may well indicate areas that he didn't want them to visit on that particular occasion due to its sensitivity to the shoot. This restriction of course would inevitably be seasonal and this area would in turn become available to them at other times of the year. In addition, they would have to police the estate themselves to prevent illegal coursing taking place, finally understanding that if there wasn't a significant decrease in the number of poaching incidents on the estate, permission would be completely withdrawn. This, my prospective employer explained to me, was working extremely well with numbers of hares on the estate being controlled by organised, well-run coursing events which were now regularly taking place, with respect being shown by all parties for all estate land, buildings and equipment. So it was important, he explained, that I understood this before taking up my new post, as this agreement was to remain in place, and if I did have any problem with lurchers this may not in fact be the right job for me! He had no idea of my interests or of how much I approved. I thought it to be an excellent solution to their former problem and had nothing but admiration for the forward-thinking and trust being shown.

So I attended the second interview in Scotland secure in the knowledge that I had at least one job offer. Nevertheless, I felt it would be both impolite and narrow-minded not to attend and see what was on offer before making my final decision should I indeed be ultimately fortunate enough to get the opportunity to choose.

As soon as I arrived on this Scottish estate I was so glad that I had decided to make the long journey. I loved the wild scenery and instantly recognised that this was different from anything I had experienced before. The temperature, the terrain, the hills (although in Devon we would call them mountains), the walls. Gone were the thick hedges of home, replaced by miles and miles of walls. As I was chauffeured around my prospective beat, stopping at various vantage points along the way, there were rabbits everywhere on the edges of the woods, against the walls on the hill ground. Here was a population the likes of which I had never seen before. When the conversation presented the opportunity I enquired about the abundance of rabbits, only to be told that the existing keepers occasionally went out and shot a few but didn't really bother with them. I was staggered. With the rest of the interview concluded I travelled the 450 miles home; after about two miles I had already made my mind up that, if I was offered the chance, Scotland was where I wanted to come.

I was indeed fortunate enough to be offered the job and gratefully accepted, so unfortunately never got to witness first-hand the hare-coursing arrangement in Hampshire.

On the long return journey north to take up this position, we stopped at a service station to take a break. I took Carmen across to a grassed verge area to stretch her legs. She was on a lead which we only ever normally used at night when we were lamping. She had not been into a town for at least the last three or four years and I thought how out of place she looked. As I looked at her with these thoughts in mind her lead suddenly went tight. Following the line of her gaze, I could see the focus of her attention: a rabbit, clearly far more adapted to these surroundings than her, was feeding against an area of bramble at the top of a bank undeterred by the cars and lorries that passed by. As much as I was tempted, I dared not let her have a go. She would not have either understood or allowed for the traffic, and the risk of her getting hurt was far too high.

We arrived at our new Scottish home in the early afternoon during the first week of February, and the first thing I noticed was that it was already getting dark. The first thing my new work colleagues who had kindly assembled to help us unload noticed was that I had brought a lurcher with me. "What is that?" enquired the head keeper. "This is Carmen," I said as she jumped out of the back of my car. "Us keepers don't have that kind of dog up here," he said. "Well, I do," was my immediate and non-negotiable answer. That sorted that out very quickly. I noticed the glances exchanged between them after this short, definite interaction, but no words were spoken and Carmen was not mentioned again.

Very quickly possessions were unloaded, unpacked and a new life began. As daylight broke the following morning it found me already out walking and exploring my new beat. Carmen accounted for both her first and second Scottish rabbits as we walked along the wall that formed the boundary between the top of a wood and the open pasture we were in, both choosing to sit up straight watching our approach for too long before making a run for the woodland edge, both paying the price for being unable to clear the wall fast enough with her in such close attendance. I was torn between wanting to spend the day rabbiting and satisfying my curiosity about the pheasant drives that I had been employed to look after. I walked on a little further before noticing a hare in the next field. This was too much: I was surely in Heaven. I decided that we would try and get a run on the hare before concentrating on what I really should be doing. We walked on to the open gap in the dividing wall between the two fields; there had been a gate hanging there at some point in the past but it appeared now to be long gone. Carmen saw the hare immediately as she went through the gap first. She made her move; she was instinctively trying to keep low until the hare noticed her, at which point it started unhurriedly to move away, appearing to be so confident in its own running ability that it was not overly concerned by Carmen's approach. Carmen gave up her particular chosen tactic of keeping low and the chase was on. Three times she turned him: each time, the hare was getting nearer to a break in the wall that I assumed he saw as his escape route. On the fourth turn the hare clearly decided that he was in more trouble than he had first anticipated: both his ears went flat as he went into top gear. He reached his intended exit and went through the gap that appeared to open out onto rough ground. I later came to realise that if I was to fit in up here, that type of ground was referred to locally as hill ground. Carmen was neither gaining nor losing ground, but had clearly come up against a strong hare who knew exactly where he was. Together they went out of sight through some clear-bottomed birch scrub, which had been grazed bare by cattle. They were not seen together again; how that run had concluded I didn't know, but one thing that was certain was that Carmen hadn't caught this one. She came back very matter-of-fact. She knew that my reaction would be the same; I knew she always tried her hardest and when she missed I would never be disappointed in her. She had nothing to prove to me. We stood still for a short while to let her regain her breath and get her tongue back in. I looked across what I saw as a valley, but was – to give it its correct Scottish title – a glen. I was going to like it here.

That particular day was spent investigating as much of my new beat as possible: every corner that I turned seemed to hold more rabbits. This was a massive bonus to me. I had to remind myself that I was getting paid for being here: things could not have been better.

The first opportunity of working alongside the other keepers on the shoot came when we started catching up the hens. Having completed our individual rounds emptying the catchers, we would meet up in a big barn and settle down to brail, and inspect the caught birds destined for the laying pens. This presented the opportunity to start to get to know each other, and soon the conversation turned to my arrival day and Carmen. Carmen was lying close by at this time without being so close as to stress any of the crated birds, knowing from experience to keep back out of the way a little at times like these.

These particular Scottish keepers' views of lurchers appeared very Victorian and misinformed: their questions revealed their ignorance on the subject. Carmen just continued to be herself: to the amazement of the other keepers, she respected pheasants fully and, to be perfectly honest. she did not find them of any particular interest. Even on shoot days when a drive was reaching its conclusion and a mass of birds had been gathered into the flushing point area once it became apparent that there was nothing other than pheasants present, she would lie down with indifference to proceedings in some comfy spot and struggle to concern herself with what everyone else was intently concentrating on doing.

We once had someone come to video a shoot day back in Devon who, in trying to get a good balance of the day, had come into the beating line to record what went on. When we watched his recording at the end of the day at one particular flushing point he had unwittingly captured Carmen snoozing, having located a nice spot where the winter sun shone through the trees; the sound of frantic gunfire in the background spoke for itself regarding what was occurring all around her. This was of no concern to her: she knew her role.

The first night I set off to go lamping in Scotland I knew I was going to see a lot of rabbits; I expected to see a density that I had never seen before. Despite all these expectations and with all the years of experience specialising in rabbits that I had under my belt, nothing prepared me for what I actually saw: there were hundreds. Perhaps over the years I had seen this type of population density but only ever in small pockets: here it was spread across acres and acres.

Carmen ran rabbit after rabbit: I just could not believe that nobody here appeared to do anything serious about them. The reaction of these rabbits to the lamp confirmed that they were rarely disturbed. Anyway, that was now about to change.

Carmen had always been good at dealing with squatters, and one field in particular that we went in had at some time in its recent history been reseeded, but unsurprisingly there appeared now to be more weeds than grass. This created a lot of taller clumps that encouraged the rabbits more than ever to sit tight. She picked them up out of their seats without barely using any energy. We carried on; each field that we left, the catch was laid on the top of the wall beside the gate to be collected on the quad later. When one did bolt for home the wall boundary was a real disadvantage for them: they had to navigate a way to a gap or a hole with no room for error, something that seemed to be beyond their capability with Carmen for company. We were amassing quite a night's catch and for someone with my level of interest in rabbiting this was the stuff of dreams.

Later in the night on one of her runs, whether Carmen had imagined that she was back amongst Devon's hedges for a moment or whether she, too, had just got carried away with the occasion I don't know, but she made a lunge at an escaping rabbit. She caught her rabbit but hit the wall very hard: I feared the worst as she limped back towards me and our night came to a sudden, abrupt end. I gave her a moment to recover in which there was notable improvement: this suggested to me that it was not anything serious, but nevertheless she had definitely hurt herself.

Our night stopped there and then. This injury later proved to be nothing too serious at all, and after limping for a couple of days she was soon back to normal again. Looking back at that incident, it actually proved in the fullness of time to have been beneficial because, although perhaps not seeming like it at the time, she never made that mistake again and instead learnt how to use the walls to her advantage whilst always remaining restrained; she realised she could not dive into a wall in the same manner that she did when faced by a hedge.

The night's catch was collected by using the quad bike whilst Carmen lay at home injured but well fed in a deep bed of straw.

Had we continued that night, our first night's lamping in Scotland, Carmen would have without doubt surpassed her highest number catch in one night. This was purely incidental to me; I was just relieved that her injury did not appear to be as bad as I had first feared.

As I went along picking up the rabbits, between trying to remember my way around in the dark on unfamiliar ground, I thought back to our first couple of seasons together when she would keep catching rabbits along the Devonshire cliffs and how I would struggle to carry them all, having nowhere to leave them from where they could be collected. Now here I was years later in Scotland surrounded by masses of rabbits with the use of a quad to pick them all up with, and getting paid for it.

With all the rabbits collected and paunched I stood alone in the darkness and admired the irregular silhouette of the mountain tops looming high above. It was very still and quiet: the one thing that I immediately realised was missing from a moment such as this was the sound of the sea. The sea had so often been our clifftop backdrop on our lamping excursions: now here, miles away from both Devon and the coast, there was just silence.

I could not afford to let this opportunity pass me by: I was going to make the most of this fortunate set of circumstances.

The following day a game dealer was located nearby who would happily buy all of our catches without limit. We were in business.

After being in Scotland for about a week I was summoned to the estate office: the ground rules of the estate were laid out to me. Surprisingly, the pheasant shoot was not of particular interest to the estate manager or, as he was known, the 'Factor'. He said that all keepers were expected to help on the grouse moor on shoot days, all keepers were issued with an annual licence to control merganser and goosander in the river, and all keepers were allowed to take deer for their own table but not to be sold or gifted away. Then he arrived at my particular interest and said that, whilst he knew that present gamekeepers were never overly concerned about the rabbit and hare population, any help in controlling their numbers would be very much appreciated, as the hill shepherds were constantly complaining. I told him of my amazement at the numbers I had already seen, and said that I would be happy to help as much as possible.

So now, perhaps belatedly, knowing where we all stood, I started to plan a rabbiting campaign, to which I would attend as my other duties permitted. Our ground comprised of basically pasture-bottomed valleys leading up to woods, primarily spruce of varying dimensions, with walled upper boundaries that led once more out into walled pastures that presumably had been historically claimed from the hill. These fields where in most cases two or three wide-ranging in size between roughly 15-20 acres up to 30-40 acres, each individually walled and eventually leading up to a walled boundary which separated the fields from the hill. This was officially my beat boundary from the lower side as above the wall was considered hill and, as such, was grouse moor: this was irrelevant as neither I nor the grouse keeper, who became a great friend, respected the boundary if occasion required us to cross it.

Shortly after my initial meeting with the Factor I was once again summoned to the office. Due to my obvious willingness to help with the rabbits and hares, evidently a forester from another part of the estate had voiced concern at terrible damage to a recently planted young wood that was being caused by hares – could I help? I was issued with all the relevant maps and subsequently went to conduct a daytime site inspection of the ground.

As I walked around the edge of the recently planted wood, the unmistakable sound of a hare crying rang out. I looked in the direction from where it was coming initially: there was nothing. But then Carmen jumped out of what to me looked to be a very oversized drainage ditch carrying her catch. I have no idea exactly what had happened or how this happened but we had our first in the bag, and as far as I was concerned we hadn't even started, although Carmen clearly did not share my view as to why we were there, because she had already started her cull. There were indeed a lot of hare damage signs and I felt it a good opportunity to make a good first impression here in Scotland. I needed to attend to this problem immediately and make it a priority.

Later, on leaving the young plantation, we went out into a neighbouring field. Immediately a hare sprang up from his wall-sheltered seat: Carmen was right on top of him. No sporting lead given here: we were doing a job. The hare was determined to get into the wood that we were just coming out of by means of the gateway I was standing in, I was determined that he wouldn't be doing this. My preference was for him to stay out in the grass field where Carmen would have a much better chance of making a catch and so took up a goalkeeper-style stance in the gateway. Carmen was always just behind him, her nose never more than a matter of inches from his tail; with me blocking his intended escape route and him adamant that the gate was his only option, a run of short bursts and tight turns took place, Carmen quickly ending proceedings with one accurate strike of her long neck. I loved to see the action at such close range: you could see every muscle in her body working together. Although she was rough-coated, her physique was such that her coat couldn't conceal her power, and the second hare was in the bag. The purpose of our afternoon visit had been just to get familiar with this area of ground which, up until now, had been completely unknown to me as it had nothing at all to do with my pheasant beat which was several miles away; we had now almost unintentionally already accounted for two of the troublesome hares.

We walked the remaining area and a future plan of attack was devised. As we started to circle back towards the truck a rough area in one of the top fields caught my eye. If I was a hare that is where I would spend my days, I thought to myself, and it just had to be checked out before we left. Carmen, as she often was, appeared to be one step in front of me and reached the area first. I could tell immediately that she had a scent and stood and watched her follow it. A snipe flew up and momentarily drew her attention, but soon her nose was back down and aiming towards the wall. Suddenly there was movement: she lunged to her side and without a single running stride she took the first blue hare that I had ever seen. It really hadn't done itself any justice and appeared to have been overconfident in its ability to avoid detection by keeping still.

Carmen presented me with the hare which I had not expected or even considered that we might see, but it was a very welcome bonus. Further inspection of the animal showed that it was not at all in good health, and so it became much clearer how it had been so easy for her to catch it. Regardless of this sad fact, Carmen had taken her first blue hare, albeit by default.

Back on my pheasant beat I soon learnt my way around, and considered that pheasant keepering here was likely to be a lot easier than what I had become used to in Devon. There were several reasons for this line of thought, one of which was that my beat boundary was completely surrounded by grouse moor, so any fox was going to have to get past the conscientious grouse keepers first to get in amongst the pheasants: this of course they occasionally did, but very few in comparison with what I was used to. Nevertheless, snare lines were set up to account for those that did get through, and at each end of the beat I set up a midden on the hill ground.

This was a new form of snaring to me that the grouse keepers used all the time, not having the benefit of well-defined runs through hedges and under fences that I had become accustomed to in Devon. Any rabbit paunch, vermin killed or dead lambs would be thrown into the middle of these areas which, with their thick walls of brush and branches surrounding them, would cause the fox to circle in an attempt to find an easy way in. This known habit would be taken advantage of with snares set accordingly and gaps would then also be created which would permit access into the midden were it not for the snares that were also placed there. This method was very effective on these isolated Scottish hills but perhaps would not be so tolerated or suitable on ground used, or close to ground used, by others – walkers and horse riders, for example, would very soon be complaining of the smell because these areas didn't just smell, they truly stank, but this was fundamental to their success.

One morning, driving the quad up to check and replenish a midden, I could see something that I couldn't immediately identify from a distance. It was a wheaten colour and appeared quite big and looked as though it could be caught in one of the snares. As I got closer it stood up, and unbelievably it was a lurcher! What on earth was this doing here? My initial thought was that perhaps it had been lost by poachers during the night and eventually they had given up searching and abandoned it.

I went to him as it was a dog and could immediately see that it was both friendly and had been well looked after. I turned the rope I carried on the quad into a lead and placed it over his head before relieving him of his snare collar: he was completely at ease and not injured in any way.

Having attended to my real reason for visiting the midden I examined him. He really was a beauty: physically he did not appear to have a weakness with lovely, compact, strong toes, and a long back which complemented his seemingly perfect conformation. I was amazed at this whole incident.

I got back on the quad, still holding his lead, and found that he was quite happy to run beside the quad. I aimed down to the croft at the bottom of the glen to see if the shepherd who lived there could throw any light on the matter. As I approached the yard having heard me coming, he was already standing outside his lambing polytunnel watching my approach.

"What are you doing with that thing?" is a polite way of putting what he said in his broad Scottish accent. He said it as if he knew this dog, I thought. "Do you know anything about this dog?" I asked, already sensing that he clearly did.

"Aye, I den a ken its name but ken yon Cleaugh it will be from there, there was another yin but yon got riover." "Are you sure?" "Aye!"

Feeling pleased with not only finding out where this beautiful dog had come from, but also the fact that I had actually understood what the shepherd had said, I set off for home to get the truck in order to return him to his rightful owner, and whilst doing so to see if I could fill in the gaps of how it had come to be there in the first place.

What had been described as the other side of the hill turned out to be a four-mile drive by road? I followed the instructions that I thought I had understood, but that only led me to a stately home. That couldn't be right, so I carried on further, eventually deciding that I had got it all completely wrong. I turned around and headed back. As I passed the stately home I noticed a sign tucked up underneath an overhanging shrub that from the other direction had been invisible. Cleaugh, that was the name I was looking for: this was the place after all. I certainly had not expected that; not many lurchers live in places like this. I knocked on the door which was subsequently opened by a gentleman who not only looked but talked like your typical country squire. It immediately became clear that the dog did indeed belong to them and they were clearly very grateful to get him back. They explained that their daughter had been going out with a gardener "dreadful chap, what" who had eventually been persuaded to clear off, but in doing so had left his dog behind with them: the squire's wife, it seemed, idolised the dog. This immediately quashed the thought that was already formulating in my head to offer to give him a good home: that was clearly going to be out of the question. They explained that periodically the dog would go off on his own and would very often return with a rabbit or a hare.

That I found very interesting and in no way surprising. I explained to them for the dog's safety it would now be better to ensure that this habit stopped, as next time he may not be so lucky. They assured me they would: in doing so I realised that, if they did as they said (and I expected that they would), I actually stood to make myself very popular with the shepherd who had voiced his own opinion on what should become of the dog due to its constantly being on the hill amongst the sheep. Even though the dog had never actually touched one, his plan had not included taking the dog home.

The squire offered a reward for my "darn good show" which I declined and as I left, the squire's parting comment was if ever he could be of help to me in return, not to hesitate to ask. I left thinking what a surprising and unexpected start to the day that had been and began the drive back.

As I drove along I thought about this dog and the fact that for quite some time I had been considering having a litter of pups from Carmen before she got too old. If I did go ahead with that plan, that dog would be a perfect sire, I felt. The thought was in my mind all day. That evening I returned to see the squire to see if he would allow me to use him. He would be delighted feel free and there would certainly be no charge "old boy"!

Things were moving fast in Scotland and I was loving every minute. I decided to have an all-out concerted effort on the forester's hares, as I said I would help, and then be careful not to get involved with more than I could manage in the future, as tempting as it all was.

Having made myself familiar with the ground that surrounded the plantation we returned at night to lamp the troublesome hares. It was very heavily populated, before I had been delighted that we had caught the two brown and one blue. Now, seeing how many hares were actually here, I realised that it was more surprising that we had not done better.

Carmen ran really well that night, although these hares had never been lamped before and were in truth proving simple, as unlamped hares tend to be, continually panicking badly into mistakes. That being said, she had a job to do and she did it well. Every mistake a hare made she appeared to take advantage of and didn't seem to put a foot wrong all night, taking several out of the squat, something that I couldn't ever remember having done more than once in any single night before. We finished the night with a good haul and I was starting to come up with what I felt would be a much better plan of attack for the future now that we knew the magnitude of our task. I wondered what would ever possess people to plant a crop of young, unprotected trees in such a heavily populated area without bringing these hare numbers under control first.

Whatever the answer to that question was, I was unlikely to ever find out, so I concentrated my thoughts on the job we had been asked to do.

As a pup, Carmen had been taught all her basic obedience and had never once needed to be reminded of it: being together every day as we were and had been for so long now, she seemed to actually understand a lot of things that I said that had never even been part of her training, including some of the swear words.

What I had decided to do, as it was clear that the hares were going to aim back to the plantation when disturbed, was to use gate nets – gate nets cover the gate opening: they tangle and hold any hare or rabbit that runs into it – on the gates and then work away from these gates. I would carry a .22 rifle with a silencer to account for as many as possible by shooting, keeping Carmen at heel until needed for any that made a run for it. I am sure she didn't approve of my chosen methods, but being realistic there were far too many for a single dog and it left more than enough for her to do. I felt that we could get far more in this way before they grew accustomed to the lamp, at which point the job would become much harder, had we not made a severe reduction in the numbers by that time.

The plan worked well: we didn't rush, and each field was methodically worked: when a hare went past us heading for the plantation, Carmen took over and did her thing. If she caught, it we continued; if it reached the gate net and got caught, there she would stand and point at it. Just like she did when ferreting rabbits, she knew not to touch anything in any type of net: whether she was pointing at it hoping for it to get out, or whether she was content that it was another in the bag, I am not sure. But she played her part well and we made good progress. When a gate net caught as they did several times while she was coursing a completely different hare, we returned to it, removed the captured animal and then replaced the net and put the hare on the wall before continuing.

Shot or Carmen's caught hares accounted for in the open were laid white belly up in the grass for collection at the end of each field. So that carrying them did not hamper us or make shooting single-handedly too difficult, at the end of each field a collection took place and the gate nets were moved. This gave Carmen a chance to get her tongue back in. We were both in our element. As always, every so often I would take a moment to pause and sit on a stone or something to savour the moment. Sitting in the darkness looking upwards, Carmen would be silhouetted against the sky and I could see that she did not share my enjoyment of taking five. She was relentless: her head movement and intent expression shouted out that she was in the mode and just wanted to keep going. I thought so much of her and couldn't imagine that what we were doing could have ever been the same with any other dog but her.

We visited this area several times in quick succession and had quite an impact on the hare numbers – unlike the rabbits on my home beat which were vast, these hares, although plentiful, were quite localised and the majority had become centred around the new plantation. Eventually the rifle and gate nets were disposed of as the population diminished, and Carmen was left to take care of the majority of the stragglers. This particular project had given her more intensive work on hares than she had ever experienced before. Watching her, you always felt that she would catch each time she ran: she always looked to be in control, and seemed to weigh up each individual opportunity and acted accordingly. Sometimes she flew in as if her life depended on it; other times she hung back a little and panicked the hare into a mistake which as soon as it was made she reverted to rushing in and concluding the run before her victim had a chance to recover. Occasionally she would come up against a really strong animal that would put up a really strong run: as good as they were to watch, I disliked these because I knew that they would burn up her valuable energy. Sometimes she would miss: I never expected her to, but of course, like every other running dog before her, she would miss at times. The dog that never misses has yet to be born. But she would never miss from a lack of effort: her attitude towards her job was way beyond question.

Unknown to me when I had accepted this Scottish position, my beat was part of the northern study area for monitoring the long-term effect the pesticides that had been used decades before were still having in raptor populations. The sparrowhawk had evidently been identified as the species most able to reflect these results due to its own place in the food chain.

The scientist arrived to conduct this research and together we would trap all of the sparrowhawk's on the beat. He knew them all individually and identified them all from his records and their ring numbers: in the first year only one from eleven caught a hen, proving to be an outsider new to the beat.

He would return again later in the summer at which time we visited each occupied nest site. Having removed all of the eggs, we measured and weighed them before once again replacing them in their nests. Finally, he would return a third time to count all the hatched chicks: at this time the chicks would also be weighed and measured before finally receiving their own identifying rings. I loved helping with this project: something that he clearly detected and was more than a little surprised at, given the bad publicity that gamekeepers in general have a tendency to receive regarding their feelings towards raptors.

In light of this revelation, he then asked if I would like to assist with a study which has now become a well-known and documented project known as the Langholm Project.

The objective here was to monitor the impact that the red grouse had on the hen harrier population and vice versa on the moor; my assistance was to sit in a hide right beside the harrier's nest for three-hour sessions at a time and record all that I saw. Where could I start? Short-eared owls were almost continually present: should they stray too close to the merlin's nest on the other side of the glen a fantastic aerial bombardment would commence and continue until the innocent owl moved on. I was fascinated by the merlins and how close their behaviour was to that of their much larger cousins, the peregrines, which I was far more familiar with from the cliffs in Devon. Even their aggressive voice sounded similar as they stooped at the cumbersome owls.

The polygamous male hen harrier that was keeping his two hens well supplied with a variety of food (including grouse chicks!) whose nest I was beside would come and whistle to one of his small harem, and as she flew under him, he would drop what he had brought for her. She would turn upside down in mid-air to catch it before returning to feed her four chicks just a few feet away from my boot. The three-hour sessions passed so quickly it really was a treat to be able to take part: I enjoyed every second of them.

Several times riding the quad up the hill to check the midden where I had caught the squire's lurcher I had noticed a roebuck lying in a shelter belt that I passed: he was always alone and from what I could see was certainly far from being a good specimen. I decided that the next time the moon was up and our nightly exploits on the hares and rabbits were temporarily restricted, I would bring Carmen up and see if we could catch him. We hadn't taken a Scottish roe up to now but had of course been told that we could if we wanted one for our own consumption. With our focus being on nocturnal work, Carmen rested during the day in order to be fresh for her night's work.

When finally a suitable morning arrived I took the truck instead of the quad: Carmen would happily ride on the back of the quad, but I never liked her doing it and preferred her being safe in the back of a truck. We drove as close as I thought we could afford to and then set off on foot. We approached the shelter belt from downwind, and by the time we stepped in there had been no movement from within at least none that either Carmen or certainly I had detected. I thought pessimistically to myself that this will be the one morning that he is not here.

The shelter belt was about 15-20 yards wide and perhaps a quarter of a mile long. It had a breakthrough at about its halfway point that allowed stock to be moved from the fenced grass pasture on its lower side to the wall-bordered hill on the higher side.

As we started to walk up it lengthways I encouraged Carmen to go forward. This she did and before long, I could see that she was picking up a scent shortly after the familiar sound in front of us revealed that we had disturbed our roe. Unseen up to this point, he could clearly be heard going away from us in that characteristic bouncing style that unhurried roe often do, each landing of its feet appearing to make the ground beneath sound hollow. Carmen went into hunting mode and soon disappeared from view; the hollow bouncing sound was soon replaced by a more definite crashing as the deer realised that getting away at speed was clearly going to be his best option. I went to my left and climbed up onto the six-foot-high boundary wall of the shelter belt, hoping to be able to see what happened. Shortly after taking up this position, the roebuck could be seen quite some distance ahead, breaking out towards the hill; I assumed that he had probably come out of the breakthrough where I knew that the fenced gate and walled gate were both tied open.

As he started to climb the hill, Carmen came into view: she had him firmly in her sights and I could not see how the Buck could avoid capture from this situation. He appeared to agree with my opinion and decided that the hill had been the wrong choice. Curving back towards the shelter belt he was now heading towards a six-foot-solid wall. All the time Carmen was getting closer, and in the end the buck's lack of decisiveness cost him dearly. First he moved this way and then the other, and eventually he ran out of time altogether. By the time I got to the scene he had been dispatched and Carmen had caught her first Scottish roe: it had not been a great run or anything like that, but again as usual she had done effectively all that could be asked of her and had caught the very buck that we were after.

There are times when a running dog overpowers its intended quarry by virtue of its superior running and hunting ability, but there are far more – in fact many, many more – where a dog makes its catch by just being able to put itself in the right place at the right time ready and able to capitalise on any mistake its quarry may make: this had certainly been one of those times.

Our rabbiting campaign continued whenever an opportunity presented itself. The numbers that we caught exceeded anything Carmen and I had experienced before, and being fresh from the success of our system in dealing with the forestry hares, a similar technique was used in our efforts against the rabbits. Exactly the same method, other than that long nets replaced the gate nets.

I don't think Carmen really enjoyed us using the long net: the time spent in running it out and getting it set properly did not require her to do anything other than to stay close but out of the way, all this in silence and darkness with rabbits very close by. However, she knew what we were doing and as always she went along with it. The majority of her long net experience previous to this had been during ferreting expeditions in daylight, so whilst I am sure it was not her favourite activity, she fully understood what we were doing. Having set our nets along the woodland edges where the higher numbers of rabbits would look to go – unlike when dealing with the hares, which we knew were going to largely come back towards us – we worked from the other side of the field towards our nets. This allowed rabbits wanting to bolt in that direction to fall foul to the nets, whilst we dealt with rabbits looking more inclined to be heading towards the wall buries that surrounded the other sides of the fields. These, however, held far lower numbers than the woods. On our early nights again I would use the rifle and silencer for stationary targets whilst Carmen ran the moving targets. She remained very restrained. I would like to say she never ran until told to, but that would be a lie. The truth would be that she rarely ran until told: sometimes she just couldn't contain herself, particularly if I fired and missed. She seemed to think that's it, you have had your chance, failed completely, and took it upon herself to take over. It worked well despite trying to carry out a system that would have been better suited to a team of people working together: we managed. As with the hares, the catch was laid white belly up to be collected later, and I always very soon lost track of how many we actually had. Having cleared each field, albeit temporarily, the long nets would then be emptied of all catches and gathered back in. Predictably the rabbits soon began to get used to the lamp, and stationary targets became far fewer. At this time I stopped taking the rifle as it did not justify its use anymore. Instead I would set the nets at the woodland edge and then proceed to lamp the field in an otherwise orthodox manner with Carmen, who was now working perfectly with the walls following her earlier accident.

The fields further out from the woodlands nearer to the hill rarely justified using the long net due to the difficulty in getting them set in such close proximity to the rabbits, as these fields in most cases were much smaller; again we lamped these in an orthodox manner.

The walls in these higher fields, which tended to be sloping as they paved the way up to the hill, had every twenty yards or so on their lower sides drainage gaps left by means of a missed stone or two, with a bigger stone acting as a lintel over the top. Before entering the field occasionally purse nets would be placed over each of these gaps. This worked well and proved beneficial: in a few of the discovered hotspots these purse nets would be replaced by the long nets set in the field below the one we were about to lamp.

One night coming out onto a lane we crossed paths with the hill shepherd who had told me where the squire's lurcher had come from. I stood talking to him through his truck window. He had been out for a night playing curling, apparently: he was delighted to see someone doing something positive about the rabbits and said he had already noticed a difference in the rabbit numbers. We talked for quite a while now that I was able to speak fluent Scottish! While we were talking, I hadn't noticed Carmen slink off alone; a rabbit squeal broke our conversation and I switched the lamp on which revealed Carmen on her way back up the lane with her latest catch. He was genuinely impressed and, like so many other people who don't understand the job that lurchers do, was amazed to see her bring it back and put it in my hand perfectly unharmed. This incident was referred to by several different people in the following few weeks which told me that the shepherd had felt the need to spread the word. Once again, Carmen's reputation was becoming known, even if this time the action that her name was being built on was simply catching and retrieving a single rabbit – hardly groundbreaking news, but as before back on our previous estate in Devon, I would never steal her glory. As far as I was concerned it was impossible to speak too highly of her.

The word had spread to the other keepers, and before long the prospect of them coming out to see her run was being hinted at. I have always preferred my own company when working, but of course if they wanted to see her run they could come. Given their comments and attitude towards her when we first arrived in Scotland, I was quietly grateful for the chance to show them why Carmen being there with me was non-negotiable. I knew that anybody, no matter how remotely involved with field sports they may be, could not help but be impressed when they see a working lurcher in action doing the job for which it was born to do, especially one that really knows what it is doing.

Hares again were causing problems on another area of the estate, not so much it seemed for the damage that they were doing, but for the unwanted attention that they were receiving from the lurchermen coming out at night from the nearby town. Due to the concerns of the affected tenant farmer, a meeting was called by the Factor to see what help, if any, may be offered. This particular farmer was well known to one of the other keepers on the shoot that I worked, although once again the farm itself was situated quite some distance from our own shoot boundary. Personally I had never met him.

It was arranged that we would visit the farm one night before the proposed meeting at the estate office and kill several birds with one stone: we could look at the ground and talk to the farmer regarding the extent of his problem, and discuss exactly what help he was perhaps expecting and looking for. In the process of our visit, Carmen could have a run or two at the abundant hares and demonstrate her ability to the other keepers who, prior to this evening, had never seen a lurcher at work. The farmer, it turned out, was in no way against any form of hunting and did not want the hares on his land in such numbers anyway. His problem was that these so-called lurchermen were damaging both land and property during their quite frequent visits to the farm: for example, driving over arable fields and unhinging padlocked gates. On our arrival we went into the farm and had a cup of tea; the circumstances were explained to us by someone who it soon became quite evident was at his wit's end: he was really upset by it all. We told him what we were intending to do that evening and prepared to leave. As we left he mentioned that he had a fox killing lambs further down the lane, and if we were to see a fox he would appreciate our help in getting rid of it if at all possible.

We left our vehicle in the yard and walked down towards the first field. This field was below the level of the lane so from the lane we had a good, panoramic view of the whole field. Immediately there were two hares in view some distance out, but in clear view from where we stood. A hiss sent Carmen away: she had evidently already spotted the gateway just a few yards further down the lane. The slight rattle of the hinges told that she had jumped over and soon she came into view now in the field running down the beam of light. The hares separated and could clearly hear her coming: as a result, they were now on the move. These hares had definitely been lamped before, that was quite evident. Carmen selected her target and the chase was on. A hare that has become used to the lamp in certain circumstances such as large fields like the one we were currently lamping can prove quite a challenge, and this one was doing exactly that. Gradually it was managing to put more and more distance between us until eventually the hare became invisible and Carmen no more than a shadow. At times like these I always work on the principle that if I can keep the light on the dog, then there is a good chance that at the other end of the beam the dog can see what it is after, even if it may be just a moving shadow. I knew that with Carmen this would definitely be the case. We had caught so much together in situations such as these; as a result of this my expectations of success were still high. This was a long run, and once or twice I thought I had lost sight of Carmen completely only to fortunately catch a quick, faint glimpse of her to tell me I was still illuminating the right area. Eventually the hare cried out to tell us she had caught him – what a first run for my two spectators to witness! The light by now was out and they commented on her perseverance: one of them was concerned by what was going to happen next, clearly not expecting Carmen to retrieve her catch. I explained that she would bring it to us and in doing so would clear the gate with it in her mouth. This they both heavily doubted. Had Carmen and I been alone, I would have invariably gone and opened the gate for her to make it easier but given that we were only expecting to have a small number of runs during this night, coupled with the fact that we were out to impress these people who did not like lurchers, I thought it would be better to take full advantage of our opportunity. As she had done so many times before, Carmen returned with her live hare, cleared the gate without even thinking about it, and delivered her catch. It really could not have gone better: they were clearly impressed by so many things that had just happened; things that I had become so accustomed to were identified as major surprises to them. Where or what their opinions of lurchers had come from goodness only knows, but they were totally unfounded. We moved on: each field appeared to hold more hares, not in anything like the numbers I had seen at the young forestry plantation, but they proved to be present across the whole farm. We noticed that several of the fields showed the reported scars of vehicles being driven over them.

Later we came to a field holding ewes and young lambs. Right in the corner of the field a pair of yellow eyes shone back: I let the light go out. Neither of my colleagues had seen them as we whispered between us. It is often surprising how people not used to being out at night don't see all that there is to be seen, but these two were keepers so I did find it surprising on this occasion. Nevertheless, a chance to cheer up our distressed farmer had presented itself. We quietly entered the field and stepped back against the wall to prevent us from being silhouetted against the sky when the fox made his hoped-for approach to us. Settled in position, a rabbit squeal call was given two or three times shortly after the light went on. I could tell by the pressure on Carmen's lead that she thought the same as me: we expected the fox to be on his way towards us. But he was not. A check back to the corner of the field revealed that he was still there and had not moved; both the other keepers saw him this time. Again the rabbit squeal rang out: again no movement from the fox. A hare cry was tried equally unsuccessfully: our fox was quite clearly happy to stay where he was. After a third attempt to lure him closer failed, I explained to our spectators that, given how close he was to safety with there being a wood behind him, I did not think that Carmen running from this distance would bring the result we were looking for due to the noise that she would unavoidably cause running towards him on this fairly quiet night. I asked them to stay where they were and watch from where they stood.

I started to move towards the fox, rabbit squealing continually in an attempt to try and camouflage the sound of our approach. The lamp was directed up towards the sky and rocked from side to side. Carmen knew what we were doing: she had done this with me many times before, not always successfully, but it was a proven method in conditions such as these. The pressure on her lead told me that she was ready and desperate to play her part. I estimated that we were about halfway to where the fox had been. I brought the lamp down to check the fox had not moved. He was still there and looking up to the sky: he was falling for it. The lamp was quickly returned to the sky and continued to be rocked from side to side. After several more yards I considered that we were close enough to have a realistic chance – if he was still there. The light was brought down and he was indeed still there. Carmen was away; the fox was still looking skywards. He suddenly startled, realising he had been tricked, sprung into action and almost immediately stopped again to look towards us. His stance sank lower in a futile attempt to make himself unseen, but he had left it far too late: Carmen was on him and took him no more than ten yards from where he had been sitting from the first moment he was spotted. The fox was dispatched and we returned to the gateway where our colleagues were waiting. We had won this pair over: they were suitably impressed by what they had just witnessed. One asked me to put the lamp on so that he could look at Carmen: this was bizarre as he had seen her so many times before and had obviously taken no interest, or he would know exactly what she looked like. Anyway, despite this fact, I did. They both passed very complimentary remarks about her and what they had just seen. The devil in me wanted to say, "Us keepers up here don't have that kind of dog," but I chose not to and savoured the moment in silence. I felt really proud of Carmen, knowing that on a different night those two runs could have ended very differently. Perhaps it would be fair to say that with a different dog those two runs could have, and probably would have, ended very differently.

We left the fox lying under the wall just inside the gate as proof of our success, where the farmer would easily find him the next morning and then be able to dispose of him appropriately.

We headed back to the farm, having achieved one part of the reason for our visit. We intended to drive around the remainder of the farm as best we could, viewing from the lanes. It was not hard to see why this farmer was being victimised: the land was perfect for opportunist illegal lampers. Many of the fields were set below the level of the road, and so were easy to inspect from a car window. The fields themselves provided perfect, flat running grounds for the dogs with a moderate population of hares evenly spread across both this farm and the neighbouring area. None of the lanes were dead ends, so escape routes for the poachers were plentiful. This farmer had a genuine problem with no obvious immediate answer.

The intended meeting took place at the estate office to discuss what help, if any, could be offered to the tenant farmer: those present were the Factor, the farmer, the other keepers and myself. The obvious suggestion of calling the police had produced no favourable results, so now the Factor, obviously recognising that this farmer was in a fragile state of mind, wanted to be seen to be supporting him. Or at least that's the way I read our purpose for being there.

Memories of how the Hampshire estate where I had been interviewed for employment had dealt with a similar crisis came to mind, and I relayed this story. It was very interesting to hear the differing responses to this suggestion as a possible solution. The Factor was interested in the idea. The farmer said a definite no way (this was the guy we were there to help!). The other keepers said that they thought the best option was to eradicate all the hares and so take away the reason that the poachers came. The Factor and I exchanged glances, and I rather think he knew what I was thinking. It was so different to the level-headed forward-thinking of the Hampshire estate previously mentioned. I could not see how this meeting was going to produce anything constructive.

The thought that any so-called gamekeeper could come out with a comment like that had appalled me. Of course the hares needed to be controlled, but to consider attempting to wipe them out all together was unthinkable, even if it had been possible. Particularly when you remember that it was not the hares that were the actual problem, it was the poachers who came after the hares that needed to be addressed. The meeting degenerated into an inconclusive waste of time, and I was left feeling very disheartened to be working alongside people with that type of mentality. This, along with other things that were happening on the shoot, had planted the seeds of thought in my mind that it may be time to consider moving on again.

These feelings were never far from the front of my mind once the seed was planted. The actual decision to leave, however, was made on one of the estate's driven grouse days. Having been left as a flanker on one of the first drives of the day, I knew this meant I had a long wait before the rest of the beaters would be ready to start. I lay back in the heather and with a silence that you could actually hear I was able to gather my thoughts and make a firm decision. I loved it here: Scotland had been everything I hoped for and more. Carmen had once again excelled, this time in amongst the biggest population of rabbits I had ever seen. She, as it seemed she always did, was able to adapt to whatever task she was presented with and that side of being in Scotland I knew was the only thing that was making me think twice. That was not the right reason to be here: it was time to leave. I stood up from my heather-cushioned bed; Carmen, as always right beside me, also got to her feet. I took a big breath, put my hand on her head, and cupped her ear, savoured the smell of the moor and knew that I had made a decision. It was time to move on.

The whistle blew and the line of beaters, spread over a mile long, raised their flags as one to indicate we were on the move. My job was to keep in front and guide the right-hand side of the line: I remembered when I had first come to Scotland how I thought I was being taken for a ride, being left for so long alone. What I now knew to be asked to take a flank on a grouse drive was a compliment from the grouse keeper. He would only have his most trusted beaters take that role, and so putting all my personal thoughts to one side I concentrated on what I had been asked to do so as not to let anyone down. I moved out in front, taking the line that I had grown to know so well. Suddenly a blue hare sprung out of the heather. Carmen was away: she had seen him immediately and she quickly had him right in front of her. The hare tried all he could, but he was outmatched. Carmen had learnt the ways of hares on brown hares. Blue hares did not offer the same challenge: they were not so athletic as their low ground cousins. Should Carmen get on one in some of the rougher parts of the moor, this often tipped the scales slightly in the hare's favour, but here today on this open heather moor he would have done exceptionally well to have avoided capture. The drive progressed and the shooting could now just be heard in the distance as the first grouse were going through the line. Up to now my job had been easy, with all birds flying straight in the direction we wanted them to go, some re-landing in the heather only to be flushed again later as the line progressed. The line temporarily stopped at one point as the middle of the line negotiated a bog. My attention was distracted momentarily by a passing short-eared owl who did not appear overly put out by the day's proceedings. As I watched him pass, Carmen had another blue hare. I did not see how it happened but I guessed she had taken him out of his seat in the heather: as it was so close I am sure I would have heard her run and she was showing no signs of exertion. I put it in my game bag and hoped that she didn't catch any more during that particular drive: two were more than enough to carry for now in that heat over that terrain.

Having made it clear that my intention was to leave my current position, I was asked to go to the estate office to speak with the Factor. He made it clear that he was sorry that I had decided to move, but interestingly did say that he was not surprised, which I thought to be quite a telling comment. He revealed that my efforts with the rabbits had not gone unnoticed and it appeared that people had spoken to him regarding their appreciation of what Carmen and I had done. He said the hill shepherds had said favourable things about me, as had the forester troubled by the brown hares, and apparently unknown to me the maintenance team had gone into an outbuilding where I lived that I had converted into a game larder and reported to him the number of rabbits that they had found hanging in there: would I be interested in taking on a role as a full-time rabbit controller for the whole estate? I could not believe what I was hearing: this was most unexpected and it took me all of a second to reply. Unfortunately, the Factor was not able to create a new post without the consent of the board of directors, so he offered us free accommodation in a small moor cottage whilst the idea was presented to them for their approval. With this understood we took up residency of this cottage and waited for news. Living in this remote cottage in itself was something of a dream. A typical day would find me out walking on the moor, Carmen as always alongside me watching all the wildlife that, whilst usual for the habitat we were in, was most unusual for me as an individual coming from the south. Most days Carmen would have at least one run on a blue hare: we never once saw a brown hare up on that part of the moor but plenty of blue and those that we saw did nothing but confirm to me that as a sporting animal they were far inferior to the brown hare.

One morning as Carmen walked in front of me on our way up the hill I noticed the obvious sign that she was coming into season. I had been hopeful of having a litter from her before she got too old, so twelve days later found me back knocking on the squire's door. I was not sure if he would still remember me after so long but he did and immediately guessed correctly at the purpose of our visit. We got a successful mating and returned the following day to make absolutely sure.

About a month later a letter arrived asking me to attend a meeting at the estate office with the Factor. This was what I had been waiting for, I thought, and hoped.

Unfortunately, the Factor had been unable to convince the board of directors of the need for an employed full-time rabbit controller on the estate, and whilst I was welcome to go rabbiting anywhere on the estate I would like to go, it would be purely on a voluntary basis and no payment would be made. The directors believed that there would be enough people happy to undertake the rabbit control voluntarily to alleviate the need to pay someone to do it, even though in living memory, much to my surprise, this had never previously happened.

Our Scottish chapter ended there, and with Carmen now clearly in pup we headed back south once more.

CHAPTER 5
RETURN TO DEVON AND A LITTER OF PUPS

As the date for Carmen to whelp got nearer I would go out to check on her, hoping as I walked along the path to the outhouse that she was in to hear the telltale sound of puppies squeaking in announcement of their arrival. The nearer the date got, the more certain I grew that this would happen at any time. It never did.

Finally, one day after the anticipated birthdate, I could see that something was imminent: she was more restless than normal and was very uncomfortable. Regular hourly checks all had the same outcome: nothing yet. I would sit with her for a while, reassuring her before leaving her quiet again. Eventually on one of these checks I could see that she was at last contracting and that the pups were on their way. I stayed with her and just quietly sat watching, hardly able to wait to see what she had. I hoped that there would be at least one that looked like she did as a puppy. A beautiful, orange brindle: Carmen was barely brindle at all anymore, having gone greyer with each successive moult, but I could still clearly remember how she had looked as a pup.

Carmen was pushing hard now and the first puppy was on its way; unfortunately I could see it was coming out backwards and she was having trouble pushing it out. I could see that one of its back legs was angled forward and assumed that this was what was causing the problem. I managed to gently ease the leg back in line with the other and after quite a struggle it was born. It did not move, though, and had no sign of life at all. I tried massaging its chest. I swung it gently head down and even attempted the kiss of life, but there was no response to any form of manipulation at all. This one had been stillborn.

I hid the puppy behind the wall away from Carmen's vision and settled down with her to wait for the next pup. I, however, could still clearly see the dead pup and could see that it would have been a dog pup and was wheaten in colour just like his Scottish father: such a shame it was perfectly formed but had just not quite made it. After three-quarters of an hour or so Carmen started to push again: this pup's passage went much more smoothly, and soon a second pup was born. This, very sadly, was also stillborn: all the previous attempts that were made on the first pup were repeated, but once again to no avail. This was not going at all how I had envisaged it would go; she had carried her pups so well right through her pregnancy, other than obviously being hampered by the bulge and weight of her pups, she had been fine. Nothing had suggested that anything was about to go wrong.

Again I placed the pup behind the wall, not wanting Carmen to see what had happened. This one I could see was a bitch and orange brindle:

this was the puppy I had hoped for, but not like this. Very soon after the birth of the second pup a third was on its way. This one also came out without any undue encouragement but again appeared dead; all efforts were repeated but again it was too late to save it. Carmen barely raised her head. She cleaned herself up and then just flopped her head down in the straw: she appeared to have resigned herself totally to what was happening. The third pup was also an orange brindle bitch. If I hadn't felt so sorry for Carmen I would probably have felt sorry for myself by now, but the litter of pups were now no longer my main concern. I tried to reassure Carmen but she was mortified – that was evident. I had never seen Carmen anything but happy before now. I was completely helpless in her only hour of need.

As harsh an act as I felt it was, I thought I should put the three dead puppies on the low wall in front of her where she could see them. I obviously couldn't tell her what had happened but I felt at this sad, serious stage of the litter being born dead, she would perhaps at least be able to make more sense of it all if I placed them there where she could see them. She barely glanced at them and just lay motionless on her side. There was a long gap that followed the birth of the third pup before finally she started to contract once more; again this pup was not long in emerging. I was trying to help all I could but Carmen just lay on her side still not moving, having seemingly completely given up. I broke the membrane from around the pup's head as soon as I could and I immediately felt it move it then squeaked like only newborn puppies can. Carmen came instantly to life: she was smelling the dead pups on the wall, mistakenly thinking the sound may have come from one of them. "Carmen, Carmen," I remember saying, trying to let her see where what she was looking for could be found. I realised how rarely I actually ever used her name. She reached around to the little wheaten pup I had cradled in my hands; she instantly went into mother mode, and her whole body language changed: she had a live pup at that particular moment. I don't think anything that had happened before, as sad as it may have been, mattered anymore: she now had a live pup. She bit through the umbilical cord and cleaned herself; all the time she kept checking that her pup was still safe in my hands and still OK. It was fine, as she lay down I placed her puppy between her front legs and she licked it like I have never seen a pup get licked before. I immediately removed the dead puppies from the wall. Things had changed now; we couldn't do anything for them, but at least she could just focus on the one she now had.

Another puppy shortly followed, another stillborn orange brindle bitch and after a further hour or so the sixth and what turned out to be the last arrived. Again appearing to be stillborn, but this one responded to my resuscitation efforts. Shortly after breathing into its mouth and continuing to massage his chest, an air bubble appeared in the corner of its mouth; whether this was my air or the pup's, I had no idea, but as I gently swung him upside down as I had been shown how to do by a shepherd at lambing time, it spluttered and snorted and somehow was bump-started into life.

This was a much bigger puppy than the wheaten bitch which Carmen appeared intent on licking for the foreseeable future; this was a dog pup and a real dark brindle in colour. The dark brindle quickly started to sound a little clearer when breathing so I placed him down with his sister. I sat back and watched. I realised that I felt more grateful for the two that she now had than sorrow for the four she had lost. Yes, there had been three orange brindle bitches but there could not be another Carmen, so had they survived, almost certainly one of them would have been expected to live up to something that it could never have hoped to have achieved.

Carmen had clearly finished giving birth. The air of tranquillity that follows the birth of a litter had descended and she was clearly more than happy with the two she had. I savoured the moment as the little bitch in search of a teat, having taken the wrong turn, wriggled up beside Carmen's massive shoulder muscle. I picked her up and placed her down where she wanted to be. I was certain she at least would survive. Her brother was getting his turn at being licked cleaner than any puppy had ever been before; whether he would make it after such a shaky start only time would tell. At the particular moment his biggest problem was that his mum just could not get enough of him.

I, of course, had never seen this side of Carmen before. These were her first pups after all, but watching her immediately and instinctively caring so much for them, licking them before flicking them over to lick them underneath all over again with her battle-scarred face, seemed such a contradiction between the two extreme sides of her life and personality. Despite the obvious disappointment due to what had happened, I was still so glad that I had been there with her to both see it and share it.

By the time I decided to leave them alone: it was the early hours of the morning. I set the alarm for two hours later and went to bed. When I was woken I went out to check on them. I was fully prepared for the worst regarding the little brindle dog: he had not had a good start to life, but I was wrong. He seemed fine: they all did.

I wondered how Carmen would react when I went in we had been so close for such a long time now but this was different: these were her pups. Whilst I had never had a bitch show real aggression before, I had previously had several bitches lying with their heads over their pups with a look that told you that they would prefer you not to touch. I once had a bitch who grabbed my arm and pushed it away as I tried to check on one of her pups who had a slight infection in its umbilical cord, repeating it a second time before relenting and finally letting me check.

I don't know why I even wondered: as soon as I went in I could see that Carmen was pleased to see me. I deliberately didn't touch the pups but smoothed the top of her head. She got up and went outside, presumably feeling able to relieve herself now that she had a suitable babysitter. I sat in their nest and lifted both pups onto my lap. Either the dog was a monster or the bitch was tiny; maybe a bit of both. They were so different in size, but more importantly they both looked fine. I held the dog up to my ear but there was no fluid-sounding noises coming from him. He was breathing freely, maybe he would survive? Carmen came back in, took a drink, and then came over and started licking them again whilst they were still on my lap. After a while she lay down beside me quite happy for them to stay on my lap where they were. I gave them back to her and left feeling far more confident that they would both survive than I had been the last time I had left them.

The following morning all was still well. I sat in with them again and decided that the dog would be called Moss, and the bitch would be called Hazel.

Both pups survived and Carmen proved to be a good mum. She reared them well and loved to join in their games. The pups, as well as being different in appearance, were very different in personality. Hazel loved to be first. She loved to be into everything, whereas Moss was more of a thinker and a watcher: he would sit back whilst she would rush in. When they had a play fight, Moss, despite his size and weight advantage, was very tolerant of his boisterous sister and would end up most times on the losing side. I liked them both.

I had only ever intended keeping one puppy from the litter. Had the orange brindles survived I am sure one of those would probably have been my choice, especially with having three of them to choose from.

The foster carers, Shaun with Moss and Lynsey with Hazel

I thought it over constantly as Moss and Hazel grew up, and by the time they reached eight weeks old I had still never been able to pick my favourite. I liked both of their personalities for different reasons. Structurally they were both sound: neither had anything to suggest any weakness, although at eight weeks old I knew that could still change, but at eight weeks old you can only go by what you can see, and what I saw I really liked. I decided to keep them both.

I have always felt that when you breed your own pup you have a distinct head start in forming a strong bond with it: the pup gets to know you from birth, and you in return have the advantage of watching the litter from birth and picking out any early signs of a pup perhaps being made of the right stuff. My biggest concern in keeping these two was the possibility of them bonding to one another at my expense. I decided that I would tackle that problem if and when it materialised. In truth, nothing was going to stop me keeping them both now that I had made my mind up.

The reality of this concern was that, due to their mum's strong relationship with me, this bonding problem never materialised. As soon as they were old enough to notice, they saw that their mum was always glad to see me, so they just instinctively copied. I was always fortunate enough to be considered the leader of their pack.

At eight or nine weeks old they stated coming out into the field next door to our house to explore the wider world. My two children would come out and play with them. Lynsey, my daughter, decided that Hazel was her responsibility, so Moss became adopted by my son Shaun. I used to sit on the wall and watch the pups get forced to participate in all manner of games. I would look at the similarities in Carmen's litter and my two children. Lynsey so much smaller than her brother with a temperament like Hazel, and Shaun the gentle giant in so many ways just like Moss. The pups loved these playtimes, and whilst I had never had concern about Hazel's temperament, if Moss had been even thinking about being shy these games soon changed his mind. He had to man up to survive, and survive he did.

As they got older we would venture further from home, sometimes going into the wood where they would watch their mother and smell anything that she smelt, constantly watching and learning. Hazel tended to stay closer to her mum, and Moss usually nearer to me. Both were learning about the wide world, and most importantly getting the opportunity to explore the type of habitat that would become their future workplace.

As their confidence grew I started to leave Carmen at home from time to time. This let the puppies explore and start to work things out for themselves. During these occasions when the opportunity presented itself I would sometimes hide from them, making sure that I could still see them, even though they did not know where I was. Watching how they reacted when they realised that I appeared to be gone was interesting and very revealing. Surprisingly, it was Hazel that panicked the most. They would run this way and then that, worried that they had become lost; after a short while I would walk out of my hiding place and walk in a completely different direction, although being able to be clearly seen by them both. They would immediately come running. I would make nothing of it and act as if nothing unusual had happened. Very soon they learnt to keep their eye on me: if I changed direction no matter what the distance between us was, they changed direction. Nothing was said but the start of working together and the lesson of watching each other had begun.

Carmen with Moss and Hazel

Their basic training had been given a head start. Carmen always responded to a simple pursed lips squeak as a return call. This she always did instantly and, as a result, the pups had learnt this simple but important command from day one by just copying what she did. Walking to heel also had come without the need for any particular lesson, although my command for that discipline was 'Get back'; this they did beautifully every time we went out as we walked down the lane. 'Sit' was simplicity itself. 'Stay' was easy for Moss as he liked watching anyway, but for Hazel it was so much more difficult: just like her mother as a youngster she was not a stayer, she was a doer. Eventually she resigned herself to accepting the 'Stay' command, but always very much against her will. Retrieving they both loved. Jumping Hazel excelled at and yet Moss, as big as he was, turned out to be very uncertain about this discipline, seeming, it appeared, to doubt his own ability. We practised daily and concentrated on their respective weaknesses until they had both reached an acceptable standard of basic obedience. At nine months old I felt that Hazel was about ready to start lamping a rabbit or two; Moss, however, was not quite so mature and needed a little bit longer before he would be ready.

I picked the perfect night to try Hazel. I had a group of five perfect new 'starter' fields that all held rabbits earmarked for this occasion, making sure that everything, particularly the type of hedges that bordered these fields, were in her favour. Solid hedges tip the scales dramatically in the dog's favour.

On Hazel's very first run she picked up her rabbit as if she had been doing it all her life. Normally when a pup catches its first rabbit I would be inclined to leave it at that for the night and let the pup go home feeling particularly proud of itself, but Hazel's run had not been anything like a first rabbit so I was tempted to try another, curious to see whether that first run had been the fluke I suspected it probably had been. Her second run brought the same result: she picked up her rabbit, delivered it beautifully to hand, and was ready to go again. I had never seen a puppy act like this before, not just for the way she had caught them both, but also the way her whole body language suggested that she had done this many times before. Twice more she repeated this seemingly simple task that she had been given before; I decided that was enough. The fields and the night were all in her favour but she had no right to behave like that. I was very excited by what I had just seen and started to think of all the other pups I had seen start, both my own and indeed owned by others, but I could not recall any that had taken to lamping rabbits like that or in anything like that way – even Carmen, who from a very young age had revealed great potential, could not match what Hazel had just displayed at that age. The following night I tried Hazel again. Exactly the same: she appeared a complete natural; there appeared hardly any point in treating her like a pup. Her confidence was sky-high but most impressive to me was her determination. She hit the hedges as if her life depended on it. Couple this with her razor-sharp reactions which were comparable to a dog with seasons of experience: she almost seemed to expect her rabbit to do what a puppy would normally have to learn that rabbits do. Wow!

Eventually Moss was also ready to start. He was much more ordinary in his initial attempts than his sister had been, not finding it anything like as easy as she did. Nevertheless, he was equally committed, which was pleasing to see, and he tried his hardest; you cannot ask any more from a dog than that. Moss had grown into a particularly stunning-looking dog: his physique and size where enhanced by his beautiful colour, but at 30" to the shoulder he perhaps could be excused for finding lamping rabbits a little bit tricky to start with. More and more I found myself wondering whether it would be better for everyone to perhaps find Moss a suitable new home where he would be the centre focus of attention and leave me to concentrate on his sister who was clearly, at least at that stage, the most promising dog.

I had a friend who had already voiced his wishes to have Moss, so I invited him to come over and take a look. Unsurprisingly he liked what he saw. I explained exactly where Moss was in terms of progress and why I was even considering letting him go, and with no information withheld Moss went to a new home with the clear understanding that if things did not work out between them, then Moss would come back to me.

Regarding dogs, letting Moss go remains one of my biggest regrets.

Having now settled back in Devon, this was the beginning of quite a happy time for me. Having enjoyed a successful period as a gamekeeper I had the satisfying feeling that whichever turn life took next I had been lucky enough to have had the opportunity to fulfil a dream. Now I was uncertain of what the future held. I did apply for several keepering positions that sounded of interest without any real conviction, but also let many vacancies slip by. I had grown a little despondent of putting in so much effort to a job which I had thoroughly enjoyed but now questioned whether the reward justified the commitment and sacrifice, not so much financially but in terms of job security and perhaps appreciation. I felt that perhaps I would draw a line under gamekeeping, and with Hazel's youthful influence I was strongly tempted to return to my old ways.

I now, however, had a family of my own to consider, so I knew that, should I go down that rabbiting route once more, it could not be to the same degree as before when I was single, because I had only just been able to survive on what I earned then and I knew that I could not put more effort in than I had done previously if I tried. Also, unlike the suggested Scottish rabbit control proposal, it did not come with a wage, a tied cottage and a never-ending population of rabbits. Nevertheless, I felt that if I could find satisfactory employment to couple with part-time rabbit control I was confident that I could provide for my family and be personally very happy. At that particular time this seemed a very attractive proposition, so with this objective in mind I declined the two invitations for interviews that I had received for the gamekeeping jobs I had applied for and subsequently became a groundsman at a private school.

Hazel went from strength to strength: her ability to pick up rabbits in the lamp was extraordinary and the numbers she caught were impressive, perhaps not always so much for the actual end-of-night bag, but always for the number of runs she actually required to achieve this bag. Her strike rate was very high. I often wondered what she may have been capable of had we still been living in Scotland.

Hazel with Carmen keeping her eye on her as usual

Hazel became a competent jumper

As Hazel became used to working at night I started to take her and Carmen out together: this really was my dream team regarding rabbits.

Carmen was of course getting older now and I did not think she was now quite as fast as she had been, but her mentality remained the same: she was so focussed, she still loved what she did, and if she had indeed lost a little pace, she more than made up for it in experience.

Hazel clearly looked up to her mother and Carmen always concerned herself with Hazel. They were a lovely pair to work with and clearly enjoyed being with each other.

At this time an unknown farmer contacted me via a mutual friend: could I please contact him with regard to helping sort out a serious rabbit problem on his farm?

This kind of claim happens so many times and yet so rarely is there a real problem or anything to get excited about; this was not one of those occasions. Having gone to his farm to meet him he showed me around what he termed as some of the worst areas – for me, they were the best! He had not exaggerated: his whole farm was infested. One of his fields very closely resembled a bomb crater and ground buries honeycombed its sides. As we looked out over the edge, swarms of rabbits were visible: how on earth had this been allowed to get so out of control, and how was there nobody local to him desperate to help him with his problem? That, however, was my good fortune: this was a real lucky break. Incidentally I did and still do wonder whether this crater as I called it may have once been an old-time warren, as it certainly fitted the descriptions that I have read of them. The boundary of his farm was pointed out along with his immediate neighbours who, it turned out, would also like me to cover his land, and I was asked to attend as often as possible.

Although a much smaller area in total, this was rabbits in a density similar to what Carmen and I had experienced in Scotland. A plan of attack was worked out and we started straight away.

The crater was clearly for ferreting only that was for certain. But the rest of his farm and his neighbours' land comprised of excellent, almost puppy-type fields for the dogs to work in.

We lamped during the week: not all night as I used to do, as now I had work the following morning, but despite these shorter periods I liked to take both dogs together. I ran them as I used to do with Tina and Tess years before, one on and one off the lead. Taking alternate fields we got some massive hauls. I loved to be out with these two one hundred per cent committed dogs, and somehow I knew it would not have been the same had Hazel not been Carmen's daughter. I am sure without that connection another dog would have seemed an impostor to what for so many years had been just Carmen and I.

At the weekends we would ferret the crater. There was a full range of differing size buries ranging from well over one hundred holes right down to small 'play hole'-type buries of just five or six holes. The long nets were utilised around the whole perimeter of each individual bury and on the bigger ones up to six ferrets at a time were used. Carmen and Hazel would select their own spots from which to start: it did not really matter because it would not be long before they were on the move. Carmen persisted with her collie-type crouch, having never changed that tactic from right back to her very first ferreting expedition. Hazel never copied this trait. Within the long-netted area at several suitable spots, smaller gate net-type miniature long nets were placed to intercept any rabbits with the idea of running from one hole to another and not bolting clear. A lot of rabbits would try this move but very few were successful: either one of the dogs would snap them up, or they would get tangled in the mesh of one net or the other.

Both dogs respected the nets and jumped over them with contemptuous ease, their bodies jumping while their heads always remained focussed on the rabbit caught beneath them: we enjoyed some truly memorable days.

If I was forced to say which of the two dogs was the better rabbiter it would have been a very difficult answer to find, remembering how I would struggle trying to carry Carmen's catch. When she had been Hazel's age they were both exceptional; I had certainly never seen one that came close to Carmen before Hazel.

One night we went onto ground where I knew there to be several hares. Hazel soon had her first try at hare: due to her amazing success at rabbits, I had no doubt she would do well. It came as quite a surprise when that was not the case. She was made to look quite ordinary and struggled to overcome her quarry. I convinced myself that this must have been an exceptional hare, but there are only so many times you can make that excuse before you have to accept reality. In the fullness of time I realised that, whilst being way above average on rabbits, Hazel was unlikely to ever become the all-rounder that her mother was. With a hare Hazel always seemed to be playing catch-up, somehow never quite coming to terms with them, whereas her mother dominated hares. Carmen got behind them and constantly forced the hare into mistakes; with Carmen behind them hares knew they were in trouble and Carmen was never slow in taking advantage once she had gained the upper hand.

A chance meeting with an old friend brought about an interesting project. He was a photographer who had been specialising in weddings and had recently obtained a movie camera, and was hoping to be able to offer wedding day videos to his clients. He asked if I was still lamping and said how much he would appreciate coming out with his camera 'to try a few things out, man!' and get some much-needed practice with it. I was delighted by the idea and looked forward to watching the results.

I had a very small farm that I looked after quite close to where he lived, so although the rabbit population there was relatively low, it was perfectly adequate for what we wanted and were aiming to do.

The first attempt did not go at all well: returning to his house to watch it revealed that nothing at all had come out. Thank goodness it was not a wedding shoot. Anyway, he was sure he had solved the problem and a second attempt was to be made the following week. I took Hazel, who obliged perfectly and caught six consecutive rabbits – more than enough material, he hoped. Again we went to his house to watch the results. This time, however, his girlfriend was at home watching TV. Having been told that our need was greater than hers, we assumed control of the TV and watched his recording. That, it must be said, was truly impressive: he really had done a good job and some of the close-up action in slow motion was fascinating to watch, seeing Hazel running whilst her eyes were just totally focussed on her target, seeing how she anticipated her quarry's movements and made minor adjustments to allow for them that in true-life time would have remained unnoticed. It was excellent. Due to its success it was replayed several times. His now suffering girlfriend who I think, had I not been there as a guest, may well have had more to say than she very reasonably did. She was really struggling for something to say that might at least make it seem that she was even remotely interested. "What's your dog called, Phil?" was all she could come up with and that had taken her quite a time! My friend in his own characteristic style said, "Yeah, man! What's your dog called? You don't even talk to it!" Neither of them would have realised what a compliment I took that to be: he had been out with me twice, albeit two very short sessions, but still did not even know what Hazel was called. There was no need to talk to her, she knew what she was doing and how she was expected to behave, and that's exactly what she did.

I decided that I had probably outstayed my welcome about five seconds after we had commandeered the TV, and so having seen all there was to see, decided to take my leave and let my friend take what was brewing and what was inevitably coming his way after I had left.

On arrival home from that night out it appeared that someone had rung to say that one of the gamekeeping jobs that I had applied for earlier in the year had unexpectedly become available again and this estate, having kept my application on file, and having initially filled the vacancy internally, were wondering if I had got myself a new position or whether I was still looking, because they would be interested to talk to me.

The truth to their answer was neither because I felt quite content with life how it was, but nevertheless it hit a nerve and I could not help being interested. I rang the number given and was invited to go and see them.

The interview took practically the whole day and was very comprehensive both in what they wanted to know about me, and also revealing the full package on offer: being such a prestigious estate this was not entirely a surprise. Although I did not really expect to accept their offer, even if in fact the position did get offered, I had made up my mind to try and get the job first and then decide, having heard what the job entailed, whether I actually wanted it.

The package that was on offer to us was a surprise and way beyond what was expected. I drove home having assured them that I would let them know by the weekend if I would like to accept this job, having been invited to do so.

I quite liked the way things were turning out back in Devon. I was quite happy in the new job that I had settled into, and the people I was working for were really nice. My children had started at the village school. Carmen and Hazel were both working hard and doing really well. Life was good.

But it was an extraordinary offer nevertheless, and after a break to recover from becoming slightly disheartened by a gamekeeper's lot, I was recharged and unable to resist this opportunity that offered us all a much better potentially prosperous future. The position was duly accepted and we were heading to the West Midlands.

Things were soon sorted out to leave us in a position to be able to move. This was an unexpected situation we were in, but now that we had decided to go, the more I thought about it, the more I was sure that everyone would benefit. I have never had an interest in money. I know you need it, that is obvious, but to me life has always come first. The choice between the life we were living in Devon and the potential new life on offer in the Midlands to me personally was very much balanced, but with a young family growing up, the opportunity of a much-improved income and the benefits that come with that became hugely deciding factors.

CHAPTER 6
THE MIDLANDS

Once again we found ourselves living in a very different landscape to any that we had lived in before: here the average-sized field was far in excess of what we were accustomed to. These fields either had none or at best very poor weak hedges: in most cases there was just a barbed wire fence separating either one field from another or the fields from the network of tracks and lanes that spread across the extremely flat landscape. The woods themselves were a series of small covers dotted evenly around the beat, in most cases completely independent of one another. Some had a hedge or overgrown ditch that connected at some point, but most were essentially islands in a vast desert of what was mainly arable land.

I had been employed here as a beatkeeper and was informed from the start as long as my beat was in good order I would want for nothing, His lordship's favoured drives were to be found on my beat.

The first night I went lamping on this unknown ground I took Carmen alone: it just would not have seemed right any other way. We had always explored our new ground together and I would not have it any other way this time. As was our way, we walked and in my mind I was soon questioning the best way of approaching this kind of terrain. Would it be better to walk around the perimeters? Would it be better to walk straight across the middle of these enormous fields? I decided to opt for the latter. We walked for quite some time without seeing anything at all before eventually finding a hare. We passed him. We had seen none before him, and if there were so few here I certainly did not want to take the few that were. I later came to realise that this had been a misplaced sentiment: hares, I was told, were both plentiful and troublesome and were not at all welcomed. I had not realised that at this time.

We continued on our way, leaving the fortunate hare in peace. I was really disappointed at the apparently barren land that we were on. Suddenly a flicker of an eye was detected and then it was gone again. That had been a fox, I was certain: we stood still and watched but there was no repeat indication. Where I thought we were I recalled a ditch that ran up that side of the field and the group of trees that were in the corner made me certain that this was indeed where I thought it was. Carmen and I moved in front of the only tree that was in the hedge directly behind us to try and gain some form of cover. I gave out a rabbit squeal using the back of the lamp to help me: this was a way of making the desired sound that I had found useful for some time now. Working on your own, the lack of hands available becomes a problem at times, and this was one of them.

Suddenly the eyes reappeared: the fox had indeed been in the ditch and was now racing towards us at such a pace that his eyes appeared to be bouncing up and down as he made his way running across the field. Another short squeak to convince him he was not imagining what he had heard would keep him coming. I had quickly made up my mind to not let him get to close in case he should get through the very sparse hedge behind us. I would let Carmen go when he got about two-thirds of the way to us: in this way if he turned and ran away from us, she would still be up with him before he got back anywhere near to where he had come from. Having practically eliminated the chance of him getting through our hedge, I felt that would put us in a very strong position. Carmen knew he was coming: I could feel the pressure on the lead and I could also feel her heart beating against my leg. As the fox approached the area where I thought he would be near enough, I let her go and simultaneously squeaked again to try and hide the noise Carmen would unavoidably make as she approached. This noise would be completely ignored by Carmen. I am sure she knew what I was doing: we had enacted this scenario so many times before. The fox kept coming and Carmen was going flat out to meet him. The fox suddenly suspected something was up, and before he knew it she was almost on him. He turned to run away but she was far too close for that to happen. Just as I thought she was going to take him he turned and Carmen slipped: he had managed to steal a few yards. I kept the light on him, unable to see Carmen at this point. She reappeared in the beam and the fox's chances of escape were growing increasingly poor. He tried to turn again, but she had anticipated that move and she had him. Her first Midlands fox and right in the middle of our new beat on our first night out: a great start and a good one to get rid of. I walked to where they were: the fox was already dead and Carmen stood panting with blood running down her muzzle where she had suffered a bite. "Good girl." Her tail wagged and she came over and pushed her nose into my leg: it was probably stinging. I stroked her head but knew that just a few years previous to this she would not have panted at all after a run like that; she was getting older and the thought of that was horrible. I bent down and made a real fuss of her for no other reason than I wanted to: she had loved praise her whole life and with Carmen it had always been so easy to find a reason to give it. She had achieved so many things previously considered unachievable, but now I sadly knew that her age was starting to show.

We walked quite a bit further that night and saw very little. Carmen caught two rabbits before we gradually circled back to the farmhouse where we now lived. On the way up the track to the house a little owl was hunting, flying from post to post, standing right up as tall as he could before squatting down low, appearing to want to take in his view from every conceivable angle before flying on to the next post to repeat the process. We did get these beautiful little owls in Devon but they were not at all common: here on my new beat they became very familiar and I would enjoy seeing them almost daily.

After our initial first night's success during conversation with the other beatkeeper on the shoot he revealed that he had quite a few rabbits on his beat, and his tenant farmers were always encouraging him to keep their numbers down. If I ever wanted to take the dogs over he would be very grateful. That never needed to be said twice. The following night I drove over with Carmen and Hazel to have an evening out with him. It was a chance to get to know him and in the process give the dogs some work. There were not too many rabbits in truth, but we enjoyed a nice leisurely night's lamping. It turned out that he had never been out with lurchers before. He enjoyed rabbiting, though, and he really enjoyed watching them work: he was suitably impressed and was full of very relevant questions.

I couldn't help think what a pair of dogs to go out with for your first time. I did not voice this opinion, though I let the dogs' actions speak for themselves. We got on very well and became great friends; we would later run the beating line together on shoot days whilst the head keeper would host the days.

I had explored my beat further and had discovered a previously unknown area by using the maps that looked far more favourable to the dogs: smaller fields with much firmer hedges. There was evidence of rabbits in several of the hedges, but only in pockets, and even then in very moderate numbers. This area was a tenanted farm known as Council Farm and the farmer proved to be a really nice person, very focussed on trying to make his farm pay under seemingly extremely awkward circumstances. I always dropped off a brace of rabbits for him when I was in that area and he was always so very appreciative of this small and easy-to-make gesture.

One night whilst on his land with both Carmen and Hazel, we entered a small field no more than eight to ten acres in area and a fox was mousing out towards the middle. Both dogs were slipped and away in an instant, and Carmen had him after a longer run than it would normally have taken her, but Hazel held back: she did not seem overkeen to get involved with a fox. I found it both surprising and concerning: surprising because normally even a dog that would not face a fox alone will gain confidence when running with an accomplice and make quite a good show of itself. I would have thought Hazel would have gained a lot of confidence from running with her mother, but that did not prove to be the case at all. Hazel had never had a bad experience with a fox to make her behave in this way, but appeared to be lacking a little bit of courage when the going could get tough. This concerned me because I was already painfully aware that Carmen was not going to be able to go on forever, and I had hoped that Hazel would eventually, when needed, step up to the plate. Hazel had already shown that she was not anything like so proficient as Carmen when asked to deal with a hare;

unfortunately now she was also showing signs of preferring not to get involved with foxes. It was at moments such as these that I was reminded just how lucky I had been with Carmen. Carmen was so skilful and gentle with her rabbits. She had been domineering when dealing with hares, yet again always retrieved them very carefully live to hand. But she had a completely different mentality when asked to deal with a fox: she was so brave and never hesitated in getting stuck in at the earliest opportunity. Deer for Carmen, particularly roe, had always proved quite simple: she was so strong, far too strong for them. Hazel, however, had not inherited her mother's versatility. Hazel was without doubt as good a rabbit-lamping lurcher that you could ever ask for, but beyond that her ability appeared to have its limitations.

Carmen did not always come out on shoot days here as the drives were so much smaller, both in the size of the area encompassed by each individual drive and the number of pheasants in them. I could not afford to allow her to get involved in coursing during a drive here if there was any chance of spoiling what everyone else was trying hard to achieve. I missed her company on these days but had to remain realistic.

It had been a shooting ambition of his lordship – in fact, I believe I am right in saying also his father before him – to bag a certain number of pheasants in one drive from one particular drive that I had been employed to look after. This was a well-known fact amongst his shooting colleagues and indeed most of those with any interest at all in this particular shoot. I had been informed at my interview by the head keeper and the estate manager that, as they put it, if you could ever help him achieve this ambition you would want for nothing, so strong were his reported feelings. I was told that the birds just would not hold in this wood during the winter. I have always loved a challenge and so of course played particular attention to this matter.

The shooting season arrived and things I felt were still looking good. Eventually the first day that we shot this drive came around, every one was keen to know how many birds they could expect to see. I was equally keen to not answer, knowing only too well there was still plenty that could go wrong to make me look foolish. I kept it private that the wood was looking really strong. Nothing did go wrong and our bag on that day was far in excess of what had ever been achieved there before, and also way beyond his lordship's lifelong shooting ambition. Being subjected to ridicule and suggestions of what I may now be able to look forward to in the future from the beaters, we all started to walk back to the transport trailer, I was quietly thrilled by how it had gone, knowing how much effort had gone into making it possible. I was delighted by the outcome. The estate manager who was always present on shoot days came on the radio to say his lordship would like me to go to the front. The guns were out of our sight during this particular drive, and on its completion the beaters retreated out of the back and so remained unseen by the shooting party. The beaters were full of it, knowing this was not something that I would enjoy. I lied to the manager and said that we were already back at the trailer preparing to leave for the next drive. He did not buy this story and said his lordship insisted. I knew I had to go. I broke away from the group and started walking back in the direction of where they were; Carmen noticed in an instant and came with me. I remember talking quietly to her as we went, explaining to her how daft this was. As we approached the top of the hill and came into view I was surprised to see all the guns still standing at their pegs below me. A big cheer rang out from the guns and his lordship did a three cheers, "Hip, hip, hooray", which ended in an extended round of applause. I had no idea how to respond: I had not expected this at all. I looked along the line of guns below me: there was a combination of royalty, dignitaries and household names standing there in an evenly spaced line applauding me! As I stood there with Carmen, I raised my hand in acknowledgement of their appreciation and turned back and walked out of their view. As I walked back to where the beaters were waiting, I felt proud – who wouldn't? But also a strange sense of disbelief: how could that have just happened to me? Where was my school careers interviewer now? I hope he enjoyed his job as much as I enjoyed mine. I looked at Carmen and made a fuss of her, asking her what she thought of that? Before I decided that, she actually appeared to have the perfect way of dealing with what had just happened: she could not care less and would rather have a custard cream.

Our lamping nights out were, as always, regular and frequent despite there being reported to be too many hares on the estate. I did not concur with this opinion, believing it to be a figment of the very agriculturally minded estate manager's mind. I think one hare was one too many for him.

As much as I enjoyed the sport of watching the dogs at work I would not take any pleasure from destroying anything unnecessarily. Everything needs to be controlled as much for their own benefit as any other reason, but I would hate to be responsible for taking anything unnecessarily. So in my tenure the hares on my beat other than the occasional one for the pot were safe. When one was wanted for the pot I had become very aware that Carmen was not finding it as manageable as she had before. I was tempted to say easy there, but a hare is never easy. She was showing signs of no longer being able to push the hare into a mistake as she once habitually did, and an increased number of unsuccessful runs were becoming far too frequent. Having Hazel with her helped, and together they caught one when one was required. But Carmen had never needed help before. Memories of how she had dealt with that strong population of hares in Scotland years before seemed a long way behind us now.

This quite obvious state of affairs troubled me. I would not allow her to struggle: she had been such a fantastic hare dog. I could not bear the thought of her feeling that she had failed: she had earned much more respect than that. As a puppy everything we did had been designed for her to succeed. What part in her mental development that had played I had no idea but it certainly had not done any harm. I decided that I would never slip her on a hare again; if she found one herself while we were out in the day then that was one thing, but I would not deliberately match her against something that I could clearly see she was starting to find difficult. Once again, I took Hazel out and tried her alone on hares again, hoping that now she was slightly older and had more experience she may have perhaps improved her technique. This was not the case: she, too, was not suited to hares for a completely different reason to her mother.

Carmen still had no trouble coming to terms with her foxes, though, and continued to take them on a regular basis. One thing that I found successful to do which appeared specific to the particular terrain we were working on was to sneak quietly into a corner of one of the woods and give a rabbit squeal and then wait: if there was a fox close by, and there very often was, he would come running up and present a fairly simple target for Carmen. With the woods so small she had little trouble keeping in touch within the woodland boundary, and if the fox did break out into the desert of land surrounding the wood, he had very little chance of avoiding her attention.

With so little cover to lie up in, it was very easy to predict where the fox would be, if indeed there was one about, and we took quite a lot in this way.

Talking with the other beatkeeper about this method that I had started to employ, explaining to him how in Devon it would only have a very limited success rate, if any at all, threw some light on the matter and made perfect sense as to why we were doing so well.

It was his opinion that the local wildlife rescue groups regularly released troublesome foxes from the city in our locality. Whether this was accurate or not, I could never be certain, but if it was, it made perfect sense as the foxes were, I am afraid, for them fairly easy to deal with and they certainly kept coming: no matter how many we caught, they just kept coming. I had not detected or thought about this as a possibility previously, merely considering the level of ease a direct result of the different terrain to what I was used to.

If that was indeed the case and they were being released, it seemed a very strange place to do it, given that it was keepered ground, but it did make sense and I thought it to be a very likely explanation.

A syndicate who shot on a Cumbrian estate approached me with a tempting offer to go and look at their shoot with a view to working for them as a single-handed keeper. This was a very interesting opportunity and was definitely worth thinking about. There were quite a lot of things connected to my job in the Midlands that we were not happy with, and this offer had come at a time when we were already starting to question whether moving to the Midlands had been at all successful for us.

I went to meet the Syndicate in an office in Carlisle and had made up my mind on the way that if I was going to accept their invitation to work for them, it would be on my terms. By the time I arrived at the meeting, I had prepared myself, maybe a little too much, and was very soon letting them all know exactly what they would do and what they would pay me in order for me to be prepared to even consider their offer. To avoid embarrassment I told them that I would leave the office to enable them to consider my terms! I would be outside waiting when they were ready for me.

I went outside and immediately started to question my own sanity.

What had I just done? What on earth was I thinking about saying those things in that manner? By the time I was invited back in I already knew that I had blown what could have proved a really good job.

The shoot captain stood up and said, "We agree to all your terms: you are the man for us!" The syndicate got up and all took turns in shaking my hand to welcome me. One, the only Scotsman amongst them, as he shook my hand pulled me towards him and said in a broad Scottish accent, "Are you completely mental?" They all laughed. I laughed and suspected that I may well be. In the fullness of time they turned out to be without question the finest team of true sportsmen that I have ever met. Each one a true gentleman – and I nearly blew it before I had even got started.

We were on the move again. I saw out the end of the season as I had given my word to do in the Midlands and ended on a high. I visited the Cumbrian estate where we would be based because I could not wait to look over the ground I would be working on. I was really optimistic about the shoot and what could be achieved there, but had also noticed that it only supported at best a very moderate population of rabbits. I questioned if Hazel would perhaps be better staying in the Midlands where she was wanted by a person I had got to know there whose only working dog interest was indeed with rabbits. What were the chances of this Cumbrian job not working out? If it didn't I would definitely want Hazel for rabbits myself. If my new job did work out what sort of life could I offer her? Carmen was getting older and clearly starting to struggle at times but that did not really have any influence on this decision because Hazel was never going to take over from her mother – that had become sadly apparent. My heart said to keep her with us, but my head said put her first and let her go to where the best, most suited life for her would be. I knew that was not with me.

I thought it over continually. The person who wanted her rang and I told him I needed a little longer; I was torn. I thought it through some more. I thought about the night she had been born, my amazement at her instant rabbiting ability, fantastic memories that tipped the scales heavily in my heart's favour. Then I thought about Hazel herself: what would she want? She loved and excelled at her rabbiting, she was nervous of fox, and she struggled with hare: if she had the choice to come with me or go to a purely rabbiting home, what would she choose? I went to see her prospective owner and felt that I had confidence in him to take good care of her. Hazel would have a life better suited to Hazel: that was far more important than my very human feelings.

CHAPTER 7
CUMBRIA

We headed north once more. When I look back at our time in Cumbria, perhaps, with the exception of our rabbiting years, this was the happiest time for me personally. If I tried to describe my perfect job, then I would just describe the one that I had in Cumbria. I was single-handed on a 1500-acre estate doing a job that one man could comfortably manage for a team of sportsmen who left me completely alone.

Having no doubt left a lasting mark at my interview I immediately set about repaying them in the only way I could by making sure they got exactly what I had assured them they would.

I had insisted on being given a free hand to completely restructure the shoot, and for the first fortnight did little other than walk to every corner of ground we had at our disposal in order to set up what was effectively going to be a new shoot. Carmen naturally came with me and during some period of each day we would stop at least once at some opportune place and take in the Cumbrian countryside around us. I looked at Carmen and thought back through our long journey together: she had always left an impression wherever we had been, and had always become better known on each estate than I had. Her ability spoke so much louder than any words. She was practically grey now: each successive moult had seen a slight change to her colour and she was becoming closer in appearance to her deer hound ancestor the older she got.

How I wish we could live it all again. I knew that the days of her catching so many rabbits that they made my knees buckle under their weight were over. I was never going to deliberately allow her to run a hare again. Although she was still taking fox quite regularly, she was now also being outrun by some that I knew would not have had a chance when she had been younger. I did not like thinking about this fact: Carmen had been my dog. I have had so many dogs over the years of most of the standard working breeds; amongst them, I have been fortunate enough to have had one or two good ones along the way, but I knew that no dog will ever connect with the part of me that Carmen had. She was more than special.

Here on this particular day together on this Cumbrian estate we were not trying to catch or control anything. I was evaluating the task I had taken on and I was just delighted to have her with me. I talked to her and she seemed to know instinctively my mood, just as I could look at or watch her and accurately predict what she was doing: we knew each other's personality intimately.

We walked on and as we approached a fence line that stretched from one wood to another a squirrel was bolting for the sanctuary of a massive beech tree, having been disturbed from scratching around in the field by our approach. Carmen saw him and narrowly missed him and he soon gained the safety of the tree. I watched him as he went and then shot him as he stopped to sit on a high branch way beyond any danger that Carmen had threatened.

We walked on again. The sound of chainsaws led us to where the foresters were working. I thought I would take the opportunity of introducing myself. The chainsaws went off as I came into the clearing that they had created. As they settled onto a tree stump, one, wanting to find something to say, asked what the shot had been for. A squirrel, I told him. Their faces changed expression as they glanced at each other. The elder person informed me: "You can't shoot squirrels here, they are protected."

A disagreement in the law then followed which I felt slightly undermined the purpose of my visit nevertheless. I knew I was on solid ground and had no intention of relenting. The elder man then made a very definite claim that you cannot shoot red squirrels! I did not shoot a red squirrel, I informed him. It was a grey. "We don't have any grey squirrels," my forester/barrister authoritatively claimed. "Well, I have just shot one so you must have had at least one." Sensing that this disagreement had gone on for long enough, I said I would go and get it and show them.

Carmen went into the rhododendrons that carpeted the ground under the beech tree and retrieved the squirrel, and we took it back and presented it to them. To my amazement neither forester had ever seen a grey squirrel before, which gave us at least something in common because at that point I had never seen a red. They were amazed but at least we were now getting on after our earlier shaky start. I left them to their work and continued to explore the estate. That evening the estate owner came to my door holding a dead squirrel that I now felt I had grown to know so well. He informed me that it had been reported to him that I had shot this squirrel and that I had claimed that it was a grey squirrel.

"Yes, sir, I did shoot it and yes, of course it is a grey squirrel." "How do you know it is a grey squirrel?" he asked.

At any other time and in any other place I would have considered this to be a joke, but I could tell by his face he was deadly serious. "Because it is grey, sir!" "Is it?" he asked. "Yes" seemed the only appropriate answer. "How do you know?" he continued. "Because I can see, sir." I had no idea how else to answer this remarkably stupid question. It turned out in the fullness of time that Carmen and I had seen the first grey squirrel ever to have been seen on this estate. How I now wished she had caught it: that would have been a much better tale to tell. The Red Squirrel Survival Trust were duly notified by the panic-stricken estate and cage traps were very soon supplied to try and combat the greys. I was asked and was, of course, only too happy to help. During my time there, despite my best efforts, the numbers of greys gradually increased. It seemed that one southerner's arrival had coincided with the exact same time as another.

The reds were plentiful and were charming. They were regular visitors to our bird table at our house: four or five together was not by any means unusual along with swarms of siskins which I could have sat and watched all day if only time had permitted. There is not many prettier sights than a cock siskin sitting in the snow.

Plans for the new structure of the shoot were decided upon, and the subsequent moving of pens and repairing stock fences, bridges and stiles, etc. were undertaken. Carmen, as she loved to do, came with me every day: she loved to find the sunniest spot possible from which to watch me toil. Unfortunately, her decline had seemed to gather momentum and, although she was still more than active enough to come with me during the day, two incidents happened in very quick succession to each other that made it clear she was all too fast approaching the end of her working life.

The first happened one morning as I was unloading release pen posts from the back of my truck and throwing them over a fence into the wood. I paused for a moment's breath during which I heard the familiar sound of a deer coming in my direction, but slightly lower down in the wood from where I stood. I stood quite still and watched. After a short while a nice little roebuck raced through across an open gap in the trees. Carmen, it appeared, had either found him or heard him, but was now in pursuit. The buck jumped the woodland boundary fence out into the field below and Carmen followed. As they broke across the open ground, Carmen was visibly losing ground and tiring. I did not like watching her struggle like that and when she came back I sat down with her on the grass and made a real fuss of her, hoping that she would not feel any form of inadequacy. Surely dogs don't feel that? I thought. I did not want her to get old: she had always been so fit.

The second happened a few nights later when we were out lamping. I had squeaked a fox out from in amongst some farm buildings where I had spotted him rooting around: he ran straight toward us and presented a chance that a younger Carmen would have found simplicity itself. I let Carmen go and she was soon right behind him, but he twisted and turned and looked at one point as if he may even escape altogether. She really struggled and was once again tiring. Several times the fox put quite a distance between himself and Carmen: fortunately this was not by any means an easy place for the fox to make good his attempted escape from, and eventually she caught him. Carmen was exhausted and needed an extended break before she got her breath back. Again I made a fuss of her as I waited for her to recover. Whilst we stood there in the dark I made a sudden unexpected decision that, having made it in my mind, I questioned why I had not even been giving it consideration before. I knew it was irreversible, so sure was I that it was the right thing to do. It was both the right time and the right decision to make.

Carmen should be allowed to retire. Just as I had always preached that the handler should take responsibility for identifying the moment when a dog has had enough on any individual night's lamping and should then be stopped for its own well-being, I knew we had reached this stage I had been dreading in Carmen's life. She had worked her whole life. She had been my right-hand man through so many times good and bad: she had earned her retirement. There would be no more struggles for her: from now on she would do as every other retired, hard-working individual deserves the opportunity to do: she would take it easy and spend the rest of her days in leisure. I was filled with a mixture of emotions. I absolutely knew I was taking the right decision for her. I was so glad she had caught her last run in the lamp, but I was heartbroken to think that it was all over that we would never lamp together again. Although it had always been obvious that this time would come, I had somehow never thought it would, and when it did happen, not like this. I am not in any way ashamed to say I bent down and gave Carmen a long hug. I had never done that before, but she did not seem to mind at all. I could hear her breath and she licked my ear. She had the distinctive smell of fox on her face as it started to rain. I genuinely thought the world of this dog. I stood up and just stood there in the dark reluctant to take our last end of lamping nights' walk back to the truck together. I knew that there was no way I would reconsider. This was how it was going to end with Carmen on top and winning, where she belonged and deserved to be.

The next day had a very strange feel about it. My decision had, I suppose, come as a shock even to me, despite the fact that it was me who had made it, and it was going to take a while for it to sink in. I was certain it was the right thing to do.

Carmen, on the other hand, seemed just the same as normal, other than she was stiff from her exertions from the night before. Her face had swollen slightly from a small bite she had suffered. I thought how it would be nice to be able to tell her that would not ever be happening again.

No matter what I was doing, she still liked to be there: the only time she did not come was when I went feeding. That was done by quad. I never had liked her riding on the quad and she could no longer run beside it for any distance like she once occasionally had. When I left for feeding in the afternoons I would often leave her lying at the top of our lawn against the deer fence that separated the garden from the spruce plantation on its other side. She loved it up there. From her favoured spot on a clear day you could see the Solway to the west, the northernmost edge of the Lake District, and also the north-west edge of the Pennines: it was a stunning view. We lived in a woodland clearing in an isolated house with no neighbours. Carmen was fully acclimatised to our new home and would never roam off alone, so whenever she wanted she could take up this position and bask. Should it turn cold or wet her kennel was always left open and she could return to her straw bed whenever she felt like it.

She lay and watched over her estate. Very little would make her move when she was comfy, but when the children came home from school, that was an exception to the rule: they just had to be greeted. My son Shaun does not remember Carmen, but his two-years-older sister Lynsey does and remembers her for being massive and so tall. This of course was not the case: Carmen was indeed a big dog, but Lynsey was just so small. Carmen loved them both and was always glad to see them; she had retained a fantastic temperament for her whole life.

On the rearing field Carmen would follow me from hut to hut. She liked to be close as I tended the young birds. In the evenings when it was time to shut the poults in for the night away from the cold Cumbrian nights, she would come into the pen and help with driving them in the pop-hole that they would run through to gain access to their night shelter and hut. This pop-hole was positioned for ease right in the corner of the run. By getting Carmen to lie down in the opposite corner the poults very freely ran down the side wall as far away from her as they could get and were only too happy to run straight in. Carmen would lie patiently watching and took up an expression similar to the one she used to pull when the ferret showed when we were out ferreting. Not quite so extreme but along the same lines.

This job was nothing like as exciting for either of us as the job we once did together, but it was still enjoyable just to be working alongside each other, and I could tell she enjoyed it in the same way as I did. Most evenings I would be fortunate enough to find a couple of custard creams in my pocket that she would find a way of forcing down before we called it a night.

On a shoot day we used to drive the deer pen next to our garden. Our house was right underneath the flushing point. Before the drive started, as long as it was not too cold or raining, I would quickly slip in and get Carmen and she would come with us. We always finished the day with this drive when we did it, and it was nice to have her out again and she always enjoyed it. One afternoon we were doing the drive and Carmen set off running. I could not see what she was after but quite soon after she had started running, she reached down and picked up a rabbit from the bramble carpet we were all walking on. She was so pleased with herself: her tail was like a helicopter as she proudly paraded with it and brought it to me. I made a real fuss of her just as I had when she had caught her very first rabbit so many years before. The beaters stood and watched and I was fairly sure that several of them may have been surprised to find out that I was actually capable of showing affection. I did not care what they thought: Carmen's triumph was not going to be played down: she had a real spring in her step after this incident. How the rabbit had got in there in the first place was unknown, but those trees were safe once more, and more importantly Carmen could not have been happier.

In the short Cumbrian winter afternoons when the opportunity presented itself I would often take the two fell terriers that I had out and try one or two earths. Carmen would always come with us, but I also now always carried a gun. With the terriers gone beneath ground I would watch Carmen. She would always hear anything happening below ground before I did: I wondered why she had always adopted her collie-style crouch when out ferreting and yet had never once done that when working with the terriers. Very often the first indication of something being at home was when the dog terrier Chester came back out and looked at me as if to say I am not taking part in this. There is something in there: do you think I am crazy? He was hopeless. I had convinced myself that he would get going eventually but now doubted that he actually ever would; he would make a true terrier man cry. But I liked Chester: he had a character and the kids loved him.

His work colleague made up for Chester's weakness, though, and she did the work of two. His arrival back out would be our first indication of something going on underground. I remember one day whilst trying an earth in a wood called the Cistern and the fox appeared to actually chase Chester out, coming out of the same hole behind him as he did by about five seconds. I shot the fox but Chester was left traumatised by the whole incident and appeared to consider his bitch accomplice crazy to even consider tangling with this formidable enemy!

Quite often Carmen would barely move whilst the whole incident took place: she seemed quite content for me to use the gun and allow her to spectate. That was fine by me: she had served her time and she had deserved this freedom of choice.

Gradually, of course, Carmen deteriorated further and seemed to look older by the day. She had never been ill in her whole life and I felt confident it was just old age and nothing more sinister. I knew that the end for Carmen was near and I also knew that I would never replace her: no matter what the rest of my life was to bring, no dog could ever share such an adventure as the one Carmen and I had been on. No dog could ever mean what she meant to me.

Suddenly, it seemed, one morning she was gone. I took her to a quiet spot where we used to often go together. It was a place which had become a favourite, private spot where I would just sit beside her, and together we would just enjoy the moment, she could not walk any further anymore and had finally come to share my enjoyment of just taking five and enjoying where we were. It had became our spot. I buried Carmen there alone and when I had finished I just sat where I usually sat and stared at the spot where she would have normally have been. I felt reluctant to leave her. I had known this moment was coming but that still had not prepared me for the deep feeling of loss I felt.

When my time eventually comes I will ask my children to spread my ashes on a really windy day, because now living back in my native Devon again, they have a long way to travel. Cumbria is a long way away, but I really hope that some of them at least find their way back to that Cumbrian hill and settle where Carmen is: there is nowhere I would rather be laid to rest than back on that wooded hill in Cumbria with Carmen by my side once again.

Carmen

EPILOGUE

Originally I sat down to write a series of articles on Carmen's life, having never written about her before in any article at any time, despite having written articles for over twenty years. Carmen's story, 'our' story, was private and for a reason I cannot explain it was something that I kept inside and did not intend to share.

For another equally inexplicable reason I now felt that the time had come when I actually wanted to tell her story, but very quickly realised that I could not possibly condense her life into a series of articles; nor would that represent anything like a suitable format on which it could or should be told. She deserved far better.

I have often gazed at old prints of warreners from back in the day dressed in their smocks, each with a lurcher standing beside them and each no doubt with a story to tell. How I would have loved to have been able to sit down with them and listen to their tales and traditional countryside wisdom. Those days and those men are gone, and what they learnt and knew has in the most part gone with them. So I hope that in some small way this book may offer at least an insight into a much misunderstood way of life for anyone with a shared interest in the future. I hope it may offer an insight into how much passion for what they do is held by some who may not always reveal their inwardly feelings willingly.

Carmen's story was one truly exceptional dog: of that there is no question. She was a born winner. Carmen would have been an exceptional dog wherever fate had taken her. Where fate did take her was to join up with someone who, whilst perhaps not sharing her outstanding natural ability, did everything possible to match her in determination. Through this alliance and with a completely unexpected or predicted set of circumstances, a stage was presented for her to express herself to the full, and express herself to the full she did.

Having owned, bred and worked lurchers for over thirty-five years now I feel perfectly qualified enough to realise and say without fear of being wrong that Carmen was far from a normal lurcher. Everybody likes to think they have the best dog: that is the reality of life. If your dog does everything you want it to do whatever that may be – how could anyone ask for more?

But in the same way that the majority of everyday sportsmen and women can train as much as they like, for as long as they like, at best they only achieve a very limited level of success.

Star quality, that little bit extra, has to be born. It has to be in the genetic make-up: should any of us be fortunate enough to have been blessed with that, we would then have to use it to the full to stand any chance at all of reaching our full potential.

Carmen was and did exactly that.

At the age of 55 I have still never voted in my entire life. I have no knowledge of politics and my brain will not even allow me to try and take an interest: it just closes down. As a result of this forfeiture of opportunity, I do not complain. When prices go up, I pay them; when more tax is taken from my wages, I bear the burden; when the laws are changed, I abide by them. I have no right to do anything else: I do not contribute. I prefer to leave those important decisions to those with both the knowledge and interest to do so.

But in 2004, the Hunting Dog Act had a huge impact on something that I held in such high regard. Carmen's life or one like it could now no longer be legally lived again. With Carmen having been gone for five years before this change in the law, this change did not affect her, but there was such a public outcry and a huge amount of controversy at the time over this subject that it has to be questioned why would there be such a reaction by so many if this change was indeed for the better.

The barbaric practices of the minority had a huge impact on the majority of working dog people. People in power gathered together and laws were passed. By whom? Was it the people who covered the location of Carmen's first catch with a supermarket? Are they to blame? In doing so they have succeeded in leaving the nearby town centre a ghost town. Perhaps it was the people who stood and applauded myself with Carmen for helping them achieve their own sporting ambition? Or maybe it was the type of person who could not even tell the difference between a grey and a red squirrel? Was it any of them?

We all make mistakes but surely there is a case for this hunting bill to be revised. Robbing a bank is illegal, so is murdering someone, yet people still do it and they always will. So why do the powers that be assume that with this change in the hunting law, the atrocities that they showed on the TV at the time to gain public support will bring these atrocious acts to an end? That type of behaviour is frowned upon in exactly the same way by true country sportspeople as the so-called general public, but making it illegal is not going to stop it.

If we are going to take the minority and tar the majority with the same brush when appraising any particular group of people, then I think that the people who passed this law are on very fragile ground, unless the so very public resignations we all see happen are for reasons unfounded?

Carmen caught so much game in her life and helped control pest species practically daily. She was a predator, but she was trained. She did what she and all her ancestors had done before her: she hunted to help man. There is no way of dressing it up to be anything other than what it really is: the killing of any living creature is in itself part of life.

When you see the carnage that a fox is capable of creating, regularly killing in excess of what most people would believe possible and you have your livestock or game to protect, what are you to do? In my keepering career I regularly dug out litters of cubs numbering seven or more. Talking to various hunt terrier men, who at times got called in to do the same job but invariably on un-keepered ground, they would expect a much lower average number. Have these additional cubs survived due to the abundance of available easy food? So having created this imbalance, are we not duty-bound to redress it? What of the other wildlife these foxes will prey upon: who will protect them? And how best to do it?

There is no one hundred per cent way of satisfactorily achieving this goal. A well-placed rifle shot certainly has the desired effect, but Carmen never wounded anything in her whole life. Yes, with the foxes she caught their inevitable end was not so instant, but nor did any creature ever crawl away and suffer.

I have a massive amount of admiration for the fox, but equally I have seen what they are capable of and in certain situations their numbers need to be controlled efficiently and humanely in the best way possible, and that should not be decided by people in fancy dress with no intimate knowledge of what they are talking about.

Like livestock going to market, the rabbits and hares Carmen caught were obviously distressed by capture, but she never shook them to pieces in some sort of frenzy as the propaganda filming that you see would suggest she should have. She brought them unharmed live to hand where they were 'humanely' destroyed and subsequently entered the human food chain.

When Carmen came into my life I had no idea how close we were to so much of what we did becoming illegal. I am so grateful that we were able to live in the period of time that we did. I loved to work with any dog, but of course Carmen in particular: we shared the most incredible time and journey together. I hope in time that some copies of this book will survive and find their way into the hands of people who gaze at pictures and wonder what it would have been like to have lived that life. It was, like Carmen, very, very special.